Reviews a

"A truly wonderful bool
cal information from someone who actually has first hand knowledge of what they speak of - a rare thing in this world. Louise gives practical steps on how the readers can connect with and navigate their own inner world. Highly recommended."
—Piper Cheyanne, author of
The Universal Wave: The Awakening of You

"An excellent read for anyone spiritual. The activities are very useful to help develop your intuitive skills. Loved it and even learnt a thing or two."
—Sarah Williams, owner of
The Spiritual Mystique

"The book describes a wide range of methods that an aspiring spiritualist can use to map his / her growth. It covers all the aspects and gives good pointers to someone who is wishing to grow."
—Ken Collinson
Teacher/Mentor at the
The Spiritual Dragon Academy

"Louise's book is an absolute gem that provides the reader with a means of using spiritual wisdom in their daily lives. The book achieves this by focusing on the importance of being connected, interested, involved and belonging to all that is. Reading this book also creates a deep feeling of belonging related to many new experiences that are encountered as one journeys ever deeper into spiritual mystery and wisdom.

"The book also makes it clear that the idea of community is not to be passed over lightly but needs to be accepted as an essential part of one's being, both physical and spiritual. The depth of such an awareness is indeed precious and wonderful.

"Louise also leads us carefully and gently through to a clear understanding of how to use spiritual wisdom in everyday life. She asks us to value the discovery of our inner wisdom, for such wisdom comes directly from the Source. She also clearly explains how we can use such wisdom to help others as well as the world as a whole."

—Anthony St John Spencer Rowland

A Journey into Spiritual Wisdom

PECORARO
SULLIVAN

A Journey into Spiritual Wisdom

A Practical Guide to Navigating Your Inner Path

Louise Zakrzewska

Copyright © 2021 by Louise Zakrzewska

Pecoraro Sullivan Publishing Company
All rights reserved. No part of this publication may be used or reproduced in any form or by any means, electronic or mechanical without written permission from the publisher, except in the case of brief quotations embodied in critical articles and reviews.

Library of Congress Cataloging-in-Publication Data
Zakrzewska, Louise
A journey into Spiritual Wisdom
1. New Age 2. Spirituality

ISBN: 979-8-46208-706-6

Pecoraro Sullivan Publishing Company
Hong Kong
www.PSpub.Co

This book is dedicated
to all who are embarking
on their journey
into spiritual wisdom.

Contents

Foreword 11
Introduction 13
Chapter 1
   Consciousness and Inner Wisdom 21
Chapter 2
   Shamanic Drum Circles 29
Chapter 3
   Different Planes of Existence 37
Chapter 4
   Spiritual Transformation 47
Chapter 5
   The Effects of Your Inner Self
   on Your Environment 57
Chapter 6
   Energy and How It Can Be Used
   for Healing 65
Chapter 7
   Wisdom is to Know Thyself 79
Chapter 8
   Higher States of Consciousness 89
Chapter 9
   Realising the True Self 97
Chapter 10
   Chakra Clearing 109
Summary 123
Glossary 125
Recommended Reading 131
Acknowledgements 132
About the Author 133

Foreword

by Joe St Clair, author of
The Seven Stages of the Soul
and *The Path to Indra*

As someone whose whole life has been a spiritual quest, I feel very honoured and humbled to have been asked to write the Foreword to Louise's beautiful book - 'A Journey into Spiritual Wisdom'. Over the years I have been privileged to have read many books on spiritual subjects and what I have discovered is that broadly these types of books fall into two distinct categories.

The majority are written based on the spiritual wisdom that the authors have accumulated on their own journeys of discovery and tend to reflect what they have learned on the way from previous writers and wisdom-keepers. The other category, which is in the minority, are the books that are based on first-hand knowledge and insights that have come from direct and personal contact with the invisible spiritual and energetic realms. Such books have a greater authority and authenticity because they are based on direct experience rather than second-hand knowledge.

Louise's book is derived from the latter category, because from the very first page she speaks straight from the heart about subjects that she understands intimately and intuitively. Her experience and knowledge - and indeed her own intrinsic spirituality - comes directly through her onto the printed page from a place of deep wisdom and understanding. So, she has not so much written a book about spiritual wisdom but rather she has shared with her readers her own directly experienced spiritual wisdom as a psychic and medium.

It is because of this unique perspective that the book is enjoyable at so many levels and will undoubtedly help every reader to navigate their own journey to spiritual wisdom with Louise as their trusted guide and mentor.

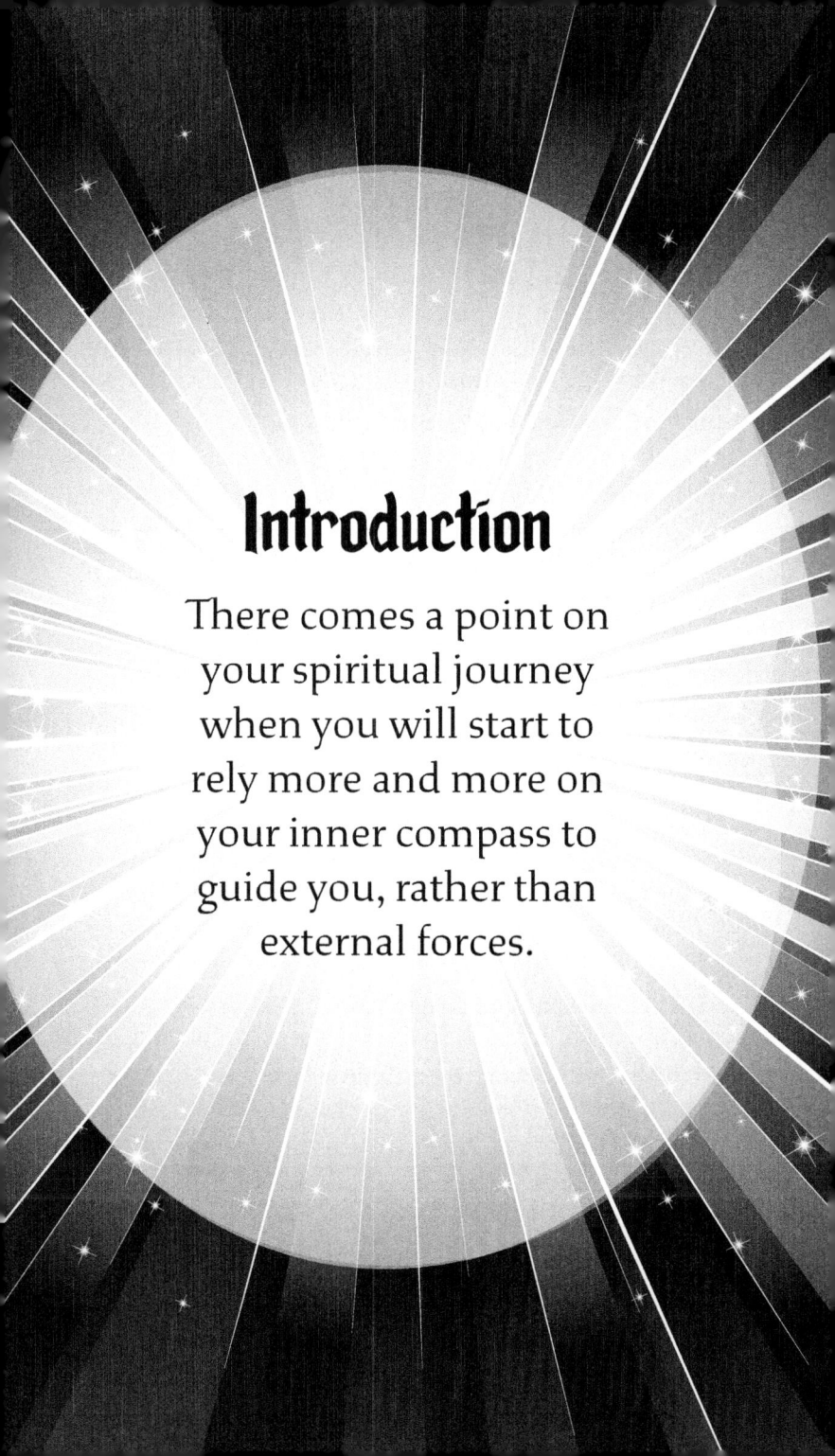

Introduction

There comes a point on your spiritual journey when you will start to rely more and more on your inner compass to guide you, rather than external forces.

Introduction

A journey into wisdom is, in essence, a process of evolving. And the body and personality you have now are the vehicles you have chosen for that process of evolution and your journey. So, in order to find the path of your journey, you must 'become' the journey. The journey is not a path based upon 'doing', but rather upon 'being'. It is about becoming your authentic self, filled with love and guided by wisdom and higher purpose. The path to evolving is an inner rather than outer quest. It is the path that leads you into the deep recesses of consciousness.

Understanding the concept of wisdom is not just about knowing but applying that knowledge into your everyday life. Knowledge is certainly good to have, necessary even. However, it is still just a series of facts. Facts are easy to come by and retain in your mind. What is more difficult is actually applying these facts to your life. The ability to relate to what you 'know' is where you find wisdom.

Do you have an ever-present drive to know more? The goal of this book is to give you an in-depth understanding of spiritual knowledge and guidance on how to apply wisdom to your spiritual journey. As Aristotle once said, "to know thyself is the beginning of wisdom."

Your journey is one that goes deep inside, it is a place where only you can venture. You must do the inner work on yourself and by yourself. It must come from your own effort and will to make improvements in your life. The greatest wisdom that exists will always be found within. Yes, if you wish, you can travel the world to learn from teachers and gurus, but essentially, they all teach the same lessons.

A spiritual journey is a deep exploration into your own mind, body, and soul to discover the truth of who you are. However, finding yourself is not just a simple question with a simple answer. It is a continuous journey of learning and unlearning; a discovery story of yourself that involves a lot of acceptance and introspection. It is therefore a process of self-awareness, self-discovery, and self-purpose.

There comes a point on your spiritual journey when you will start to rely more and more on your inner compass to guide you, rather than external forces. You start to see the truth of the world as a sort of mirror - a direct reflection of your own consciousness.

In Chapter One of the book, I explain that you create your own universe, as your environment is simply your perception of reality from a subjective point of view. It is a projection of your consciousness and perception of your observation. As an observer, you are experiencing and creating reality with a story in your mind. So, it is important on your spiritual journey that you pay attention and listen to your inner wisdom whilst observing the images the mind projects and letting your internal compass guide you.

Your internal compass will thus help you evolve and become aligned with your soul's purpose.

I also explain in Chapter One of the book that your conscious awareness and subconscious mind determines the quality of your life, but consciousness itself can go far beyond your physical, emotional, and mental capability.

You can, however, learn to shift your conscious experience or perception of the outer world of thoughts and emotions, to a heightened state of consciousness if you so wish. This can be attained by creating a 'sacred space'. And one way to create sacred space is through shamanic drum circles, which I explain in more detail in Chapter Two of the book.

In Chapter Two, I explain that shamanic drum circles make it possible to achieve altered states of consciousness to connect with different planes of existence. Then in the Third Chapter of the book I explain other ways you can connect with different planes of existence as well as ways to practice and improve the communication with your Spirit Guide. I will also explain why trusting your Spirit Guide can help you through a spiritual transformation.

In Chapter Four of the book, I go into more detail about spiritual transformation and ways that can help you through this transition, to become the 'best version' of yourself.

I also mention in Chapter Four, how you can monitor your inner self, which requires a high level of introspection and self-awareness that changes the environment you surround yourself in. Then in Chapter Five I explain the effects of your inner self on your environment.

I explain that everything is perceived through the self and alters according to your inner state. If you learn to change yourself then your circumstances will change because you can influence and reform your environment with your thoughts and what you believe.

With your thoughts you attract situations and people to your life because of an energy field that generates inside your body and extends outward to surround you. Like a strong magnet, your field of energy draws other energies to it and absorbs the power of them. This magnetic energy draws to you the situations, people and events that reinforce whatever you believe and think. It is your thoughts that shape the very essence of you and your life.

There is also a life-force energy that connects everything that exists and all living beings are taking in this energy at every moment. This energy flows through everything and it is responsive to every thought. You can use this energy for healing, which I explain in more detail in Chapter Six of the book.

Also in Chapter Six, I explain the different ways energy can be used for healing - and one way is to channel healing to a body's subtle energy field by expanding consciousness. The body's subtle energy field is a system made up of a number of layers of vibrating energy, each of which have their own specific vibration and purpose.

In addition, there are seven 'chakras' that function as doorways connecting your body's auric field. They are individual centres of activity that receive and express life force energy. The more developed these are, the higher your overall frequency will be, because you are more connected to the universal life force energy that flows through everything in the universe.

In Chapter Seven I explain that everything that exists in the universe is made up of energy and has its own vibrational frequency. Your frequency of vibration is based on what you think about, so it's important to be conscious of your frequency by focusing on the feeling of what you want to experience. Also, every thought and action, has a corresponding effect, whether it is instant or occurs in the future. You need to become aware that you can alter your reality by simply changing your thoughts. Your thoughts are powerful, so it's very important to keep a regular high-vibrational state in your daily life.

The universe is a creation of God from which everything originates. This creation is an energy flow with an infinite number of vibrations. Everything that lives and exists has its own unique vibration that is only a tiny part of that infinite energy flow. It includes the material universe; life in all its forms, energy, matter, and everything you can perceive with your senses.

You are therefore a purely sentient being with energies that are genderless in nature. To know this is to understand something called 'oneness'. This understanding allows you to reach higher states of consciousness and I explain what the higher states of consciousness are in Chapter Eight of the book.

In Chapter Nine I explain that the remembrance of God, or self-remembering, happens at the level of the cosmic mind, which is the ultimate in consciousness. God or 'Divine-Self' is manifest when you ultimately become completely integrated with the ultimate consciousness.

Divinity is not to be achieved but rather unveiled and recognised. It's your own forgetfulness, your unconsciousness, which covers the truth.

You are beyond time and space. Also, you are beyond form and formlessness. You are that which is beyond the mind and beyond every concept of 'you'. When you know the 'I', you are then able to take charge of the thoughts, feelings, and actions that guide your behaviour.

You are not your body or mind, or your senses but the inner self which is permanent, eternal and infinite that shares the same consciousness as God or the Divine. However, your actions have consequences, both good and bad, as they come back to you in the future, helping you to learn from your life's lessons. This is called 'karma', which is one of the natural laws of the mind, just as gravity is a law of matter.

Karma can be stored from previous lives and new karma is generated at every moment of your existence. Vedanta believes that it's your chakras that store the karma for this lifetime.

Chakras are your subtle energy centres through which consciousness transforms into matter, and I explain ways to clear your chakras in Chapter Ten of the book.

The term 'Vedanta' in Sanskrit means the 'conclusion' (anta) of the Vedas. 'Veda' means knowledge but particularly self-knowledge. By knowing the true nature of the Self, you then not only know the essence of all things, but are freed from the endless sorrows of the cycle of death and rebirth to which life in the material world is bound called 'samsara'.

Over many incarnations or cycles of death and rebirth, the soul connects with the ego, creating a communication bridge that links the soul with the personality. In addition, another bridge is formed from the soul to something which is called the 'Monad' or 'life above', this bridge is called the 'Antahkarana' and there is more about this in Chapters Nine and Ten.

Every chapter includes activities so you can apply what you've learnt to your everyday life straight away.

A Journey into Spiritual Wisdom

This will help you on your journey to understanding wisdom and guide you on your spiritual path.

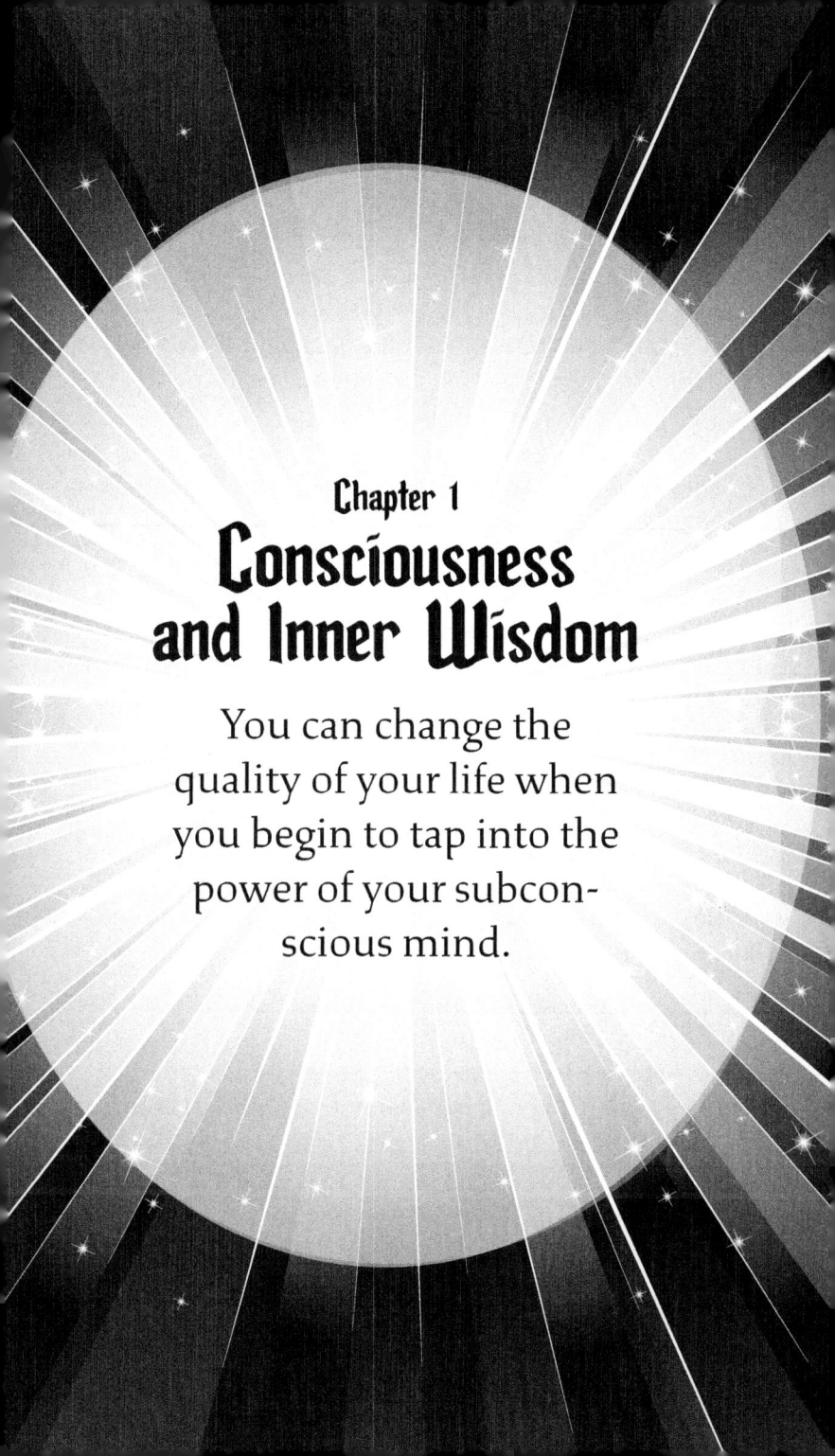

Chapter 1
Consciousness and Inner Wisdom

You can change the quality of your life when you begin to tap into the power of your subconscious mind.

Consciousness and Inner Wisdom

Your thoughts are responsible for everything that happens in your life as they influence your behaviour. And the observation of your thoughts creates your experience of life.

As an observer, you notice thoughts appear in your mind by themselves and effectively this becomes your inner wisdom. When you start to listen to your inner wisdom you see the images the mind projects. Over time you start to become aware that you are separate from your mind - and you are also not your body. Your body is made up of particles of matter, cells and a nerve centre that communicates with your brain. Your brain's system functions automatically and carries out all of your core biological processes without you being consciously aware of it. The brain is visible, tangible and part of your body. Whereas your mind is invisible and transcendent; it's your thoughts, feelings, attitude, beliefs and imagination. The mind is what functions to understand things; it is formless, or non-physical, and shapes your behaviour. However, the observer that experiences and creates reality is consciousness itself.

Think of the brain as being like a TV screen with the mind being the tiny dots of light produced on the TV screen, which are called pixels. Pixels are what your mind recognises as images that create the movie. Consciousness is the vision focused on the movie and what is identifying with the story. The events happening in the story of the movie, are like events happening in your life. The screen on which the events are displayed is like the story in your mind. Your consciousness is what is observing and experiencing the story in your mind. So, in a nutshell, it is the quality of consciousness that determines the quality of your life.

You can change the quality of your life when you begin to tap into the power of your subconscious mind. This part of your mind is not consciously processing 'in the moment' but stores all memories and situations you have been through. It contains all your habits, your beliefs, and your personality. It is responsible for automatically triggered thoughts and emotions. For example, if you experience a new situation in your life, you may react with doubt and fear. This could be triggered by the subconscious mind and its conditioning, as it determines your pattern of thought and behaviour much more than you realise.

Your subconscious mind is programmed much like a computer because it identifies with a belief system and thinking pattern. You must change your belief system and thinking pattern to align your subconscious mind into complete agreement with your conscious thoughts to accomplish your goals and improve your life.

Your conscious thoughts are something you are engaged with because you are very aware of what you are thinking and why you are thinking it. It is part of the mind that is aware, and it knows only logic and reason. It categorises what is going on around you. It is part of your consciousness in this present moment as you read and understand these words.

The conscious awareness and subconscious are states of the mind. There is also another consciousness that is beyond the mind called 'super-consciousness' or 'higher consciousness'. It is beyond your physical, emotional, and mental capability. It is non - dual, as it does not distinguish between good or bad, wrong, or right, happy or sad. It knows only balance and true love. It is the eternal observer and absolute stillness. Only through stillness, can you identify with super-consciousness. This is because with a still mind, a new dimension of existence opens for you. You become more aware of yourself and all the things that impact your well-being, inner peace, and happiness. You begin to live from a place of truth and pay attention to your wise inner voice. The wise inner voice is calm and non-judgmental, always there helping you on your spiritual journey. Your spiritual journey is a process of evolving and becoming aligned with your soul's purpose. When this happens, you start to embrace your inner wisdom, share it with the rest of the world, and do the meaningful work you came here to do. This could mean giving strength, clarity, courage, wisdom, confidence, and guidance to others. Using one or more of these gifts that are hidden deep within you:

—» **Gift of wisdom** - the ability to give guidance to others from a higher consciousness or a higher self, a transcendental reality, or God. An awakened aspect of yourself, the deepest truth and hidden knowledge. This gift helps others awaken their true self, their life purpose, and evolve as spiritual beings.

—» **Gift of knowledge** - the ability to have an in-depth understanding of spiritual issues that can help others. Real knowledge is based on experiential searching, seeking genuine truth, or just knowing naturally and intuitively. This is an ability to instinctively know the power to influence, transform and enhance lives.

—» **Gift of healing** - the ability to channel higher vibrational energy to others so they can heal themselves. This is healing of the mind and soul, to attain balance and healthy lives.

—» **Gift of prophecy** - the ability to be able to proclaim a message to help others. This is divinely inspired information that is gathered and obtained through, psychic gifts, sign reading, or the altering of consciousness.

—» **Gift of awareness** - a realisation that separation and duality are an illusion. This understanding can help others discover the truth, open their hearts to find the centre of their being, and discover that we are all connected as universal intelligence.

These gifts are blessings from the universe. As being one with the Creator you connect with universal intelligence and it communicates with you all the time though you may not always recognise the messages or realise when it communicates with you.

If you are not receiving messages from the universe, it means you need to tune into your inner world, so the more loudly your dialogue with the universe will become. This is because you create your own universe, as your environment is simply your perception of reality from a subjective point of view. It is a projection of your consciousness and a perception of your observations.

You are also a being of the Creator with one consciousness that pervades the entire Universe, as it is everywhere at the same time, and it is present in you. Your consciousness is part of one universal consciousness, it is everything that exists. There is consciousness in every particle, no matter how small. There are billions of cells in your body, which all function on their own. Yet at the same time, they are all connected to each other and form one whole. Through us, the Creator constantly experiences itself as a limitless and all-embracing whole. And you are also experiencing yourself as a part contained within a limitless and all-embracing whole.

If you truly embrace yourself as one with the whole, and not as separate being, it's possible to consciously tap into the same power that drives the entire universe. This is because nothing is separate, everything consists entirely of energy, and all energy is intimately connected.

When stilling the mind, you can connect with this energy and align yourself with a higher level of truth, so you can be of greater service and know your highest path.

Your inner wisdom is an internal compass which carries with it universal truth. You do not need to look outside of yourselves for truth and information, it is within reach if you simply listen to it. Listen and it will give you all the information, all the knowing and all the answers that you seek. It is within you, for there is no disconnection between your own internal wisdom and universal wisdom. It is unlimited and eternal. In fact, it is more than a connection as it is a unity. There is no separation from God or from the Divine energy that is the Creator of all things. You just need to embrace the limitless qualities of your Divine nature as a limitless being having a conscious experience. You can shift your conscious experience or perception of the outer world of thoughts and emotions, to the inner world of pure awareness or a higher state of consciousness.

Activities

Start each day with positive affirmations that can train your subconscious mind. This part of the mind is what automatically triggers your thoughts and emotions. It influences you and affects your behaviour without you being aware of it. Some affirmations you could use are:
"I am positive!"
"I am a master of my body!"
"I am a master of myself!"
"Be strong!"

Write affirmations down on a sheet of paper and stick or hang them in such a place that the words can be seen frequently throughout the day. This will condition your subconscious mind to view it as the truth. It will help you re-program self-defeating thought patterns.

Listen to music for deep relaxation to occupy the conscious mind with certain rhythms that make it calm and receptive, so it's absorbed directly at the subconscious level. Your conscious mind might be listening to relaxing soft music, but your subconscious mind also hears all the positive and powerful affirmations.

Create sacred space to connect with yourself. This could be a place in nature or a place in your home used for quiet meditation. It needs to be a place you can let go mentally and emotionally to clear your mind so that you notice your wise inner voice. If you don't hear anything, take notice of what you sense or feel. It could be random thoughts, images or symbols that come to your mind. Record what you hear, see, feel or sense in a journal.

Attend a shamanic drum circle where sacred space can be created to receive guidance, inspiration, clarity, and wisdom.

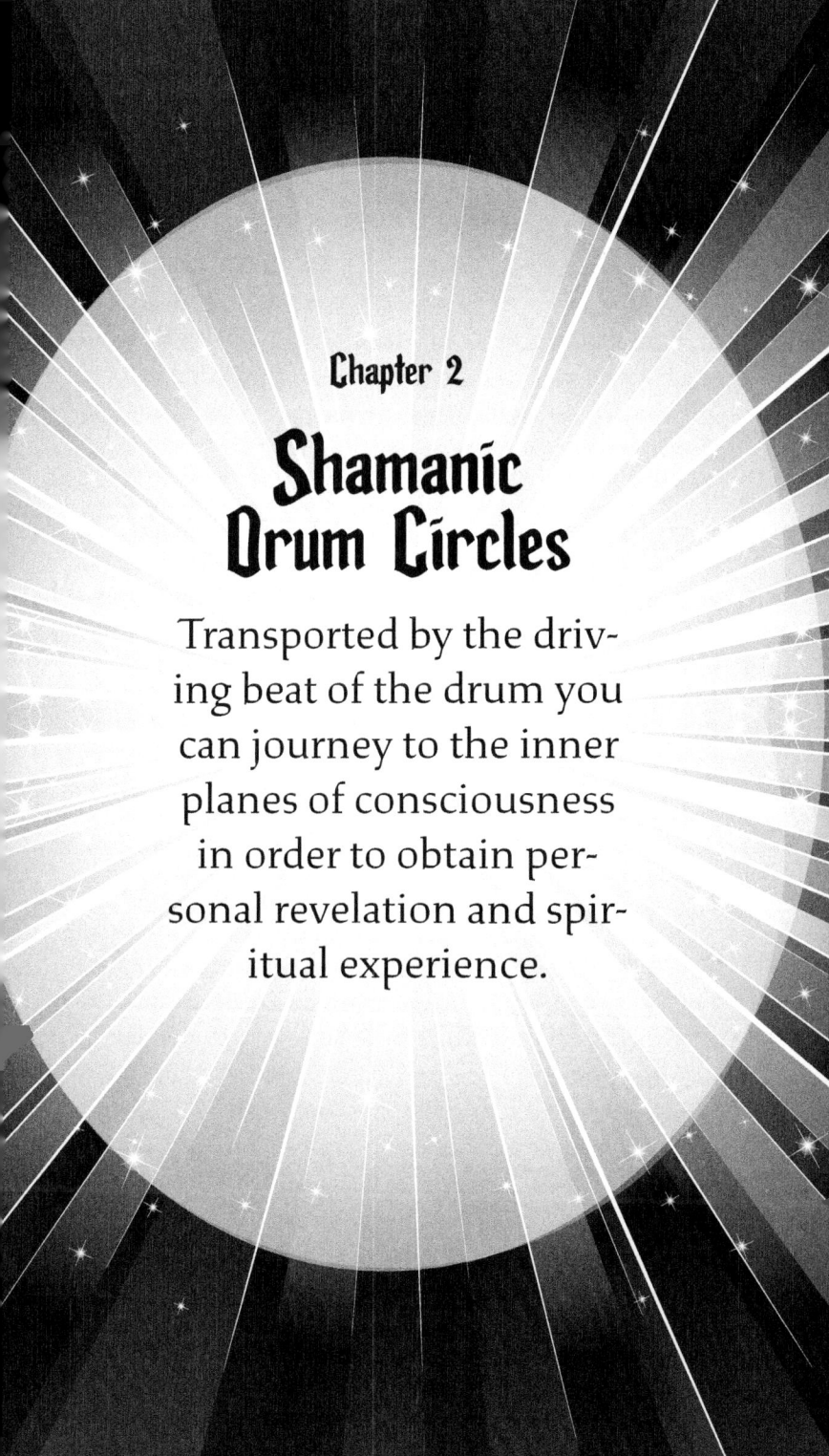

Chapter 2
Shamanic Drum Circles

Transported by the driving beat of the drum you can journey to the inner planes of consciousness in order to obtain personal revelation and spiritual experience.

Shamanic Drum Circles

Shamanism has been practiced by many indigenous cultures for thousands of years. It is believed to be the most ancient and most enduring spiritual tradition known to humanity. It provides access to a higher wisdom, spiritual guidance, and healing.

The essence of this practice is to reconnect you with your deepest core values, and the highest version of yourself. It also helps you to remember, explore and develop your authentic self.

During a shamanic drum circle everyone is encouraged to express themselves using chant, song, sound and dance to help raise energy as it helps to increase endorphin levels in your brain making you feel more empowered.

Raising energy using the shamanic drum can help you attain an altered state of consciousness to explore and broaden your own perceptions of reality, reconnecting you with others and nature. It can also heighten consciousness, increase your awareness about yourself and affect how you impact the world around you.

In shamanic drum circles you create a sacred space so you can journey to non-ordinary realities through a specific pattern of drumming. This is a constant rhythm conducted at a fast pace (4-7 beats per second). A constant rhythm affects consciousness allowing a well-defined altered state that helps with meditation, out of body journeying and experiences with other dimensions.

The beat of the drum can be like the sound of a heartbeat, which a very comforting sound because it's the very first sound you ever heard whilst still in your mother's womb. It was the beating of your mother's heart and the rhythm of her breath that soothed you. Also, the beat of the drum connects your heart to the heartbeat of the earth.

This rhythmic pulse can connect you with humanity, with all living things and with the entire universe. It is your natural state, it doesn't just exist in your body, your heart and your breath, but the orbit of the earth. Everything is a rhythm, and for this reason it can be used to induce a trance state that alters the brain wave patterns, entraining brainwaves from the 'beta state' (conscious, waking state) to 'alpha state' (subconscious, deep relaxation) to a 'theta state' (deep meditation, creativity).

Here are the descriptions of the different brainwaves:

—» Beta 13-40 Hz - Alert, normal alert consciousness, active thinking and strongly engaged mind
—» Alpha 8-12 Hz - Physically and mentally relaxed state
—» Theta 5-7 Hz - Creativity, insight, dreams, reduced consciousness
—» Delta 1- 4 Hz - Associated with sleep and drowsiness

Beta waves reflect a state of alertness and attention as it is the conscious waking state. Alpha waves arise when the eyes are closed, and the mind is in a relaxed state. In the deeper states associated with alpha waves, there is a loss of awareness of the environment as one drifts into a profound state of relaxation.

Shamanic drumming can alter your state of consciousness from beta and alpha to theta.

Theta waves are pathways to the subconscious mind. In this state the brain works at a low frequency of 4 to 7 Hz, it produces theta waves on electroencephalograms (EEGs), which detects abnormalities in your brain waves, or in the electrical activity of your brain.

A state of consciousness associated with deep physical relaxation, mental clarity, dream-like states, and hypnosis. This is a disconnection from the conscious world. It is a state of imagination, creativity and lucid dreaming. The best way to induce theta waves is to drum rhythmically at 4 to 4.5 beats per second for 15 minutes.

Shamanic drumming is a powerful experience that is deeply healing. It allows you to explore your subconscious and to enter insightful states that open access to unseen dimensions. It is a way to communicate with your inner self and to find the root of your deepest thoughts and emotions. It also allows you to view life and life's problems from a detached, spiritual perspective, not easily achieved in a state of ordinary consciousness.

Transported by the driving beat of the drum you can journey to the inner planes of consciousness in order to obtain personal revelation and spiritual experience.

You can also use the shamanic drum as a tool to connect with the spirit world through different tempos and tones. These tempo and tones are sound waves that create a conduit between this world and the world of spirit. The drumbeats create various levels of vibration, allowing a connection to either your spirit animal or spirit guide, depending on the tone. For example, you can enter a dream state, experience a vision, or enter a trance state with your Spirit Guide using a drum beat with a high tone. You can also reach your Animal Spirit for insight or healing using a drum beat with a low tone, as spirit animals are believed to be found in the lower world.

In shamanism there are three realms which are called the 'lower world', 'middle world' and the 'upper world'. The drum's rhythm can also open 'portals' between these three worlds.

A portal is a gateway that connects you to other worlds, it is an opening to which energy flows and information can be received.

Imagine a tree which represents all three worlds: the lower world (the roots of the tree) is the world of the dead and underground spirits; the middle world (trunk) is the human realm, and the upper world (branches) is the world of heavenly spirits and gods. The beat of the shamanic drum can connect all three of these worlds like the tree's roots, trunk and branches are connected. This is because nothing is separate, everything consists entirely of energy, and all energy is connected.

The shamanic drum can be used as a tool to commune with the unseen world to effect changes in the physical world. You can retrieve information from your Spirit Guides that provide you with insights. These are insights into things you must do and/or change as you pursue your own personal growth and spiritual transformation.

If you can communicate with your Spirit Guides then you will have an ability to achieve altered states of consciousness, which, in turn, gives you the ability to see into other worlds. This means you are still in your body, but all your senses are in the spirit world, so you can see, hear, and feel different planes of existence.

Activities

Find a shamanic drum circle where people drum together with a purpose of building energy and community. A circle that calls on the help of the natural world through invoking the four cardinal directions. This invites the animal archetypes and the universe to provide a safe space to do ceremonial work or meditate. This is a way to shift your consciousness from the mundane to the sacred. It's a way of creating a 'zone' in which all things will be treated as sacred.

Study the Shamanic Energy Medicine Wheel that corresponds with the four directions: South, West, North and East.

Download some free drumming tracks online. Get comfortable and listen to a drumbeat – this would be a monotonous rhythm so that you don't engage your conscious mind but the subconscious. Your subconscious can venture and experience the journey into the spirit world. During your journey let go of the need to control and detach from the outcome. You need to trust that what you are given is what is specifically needed at that precise time.

Visit a Shamanic Practitioner who can act as a bridge between the shamanic indigenous world and the modern world. They can borrow the medicine and wisdom of ancestors to help you at a point of transition in your life or if you desire deep soul-healing. This could also be done remotely where you can connect by email, phone or video.

Chapter 3

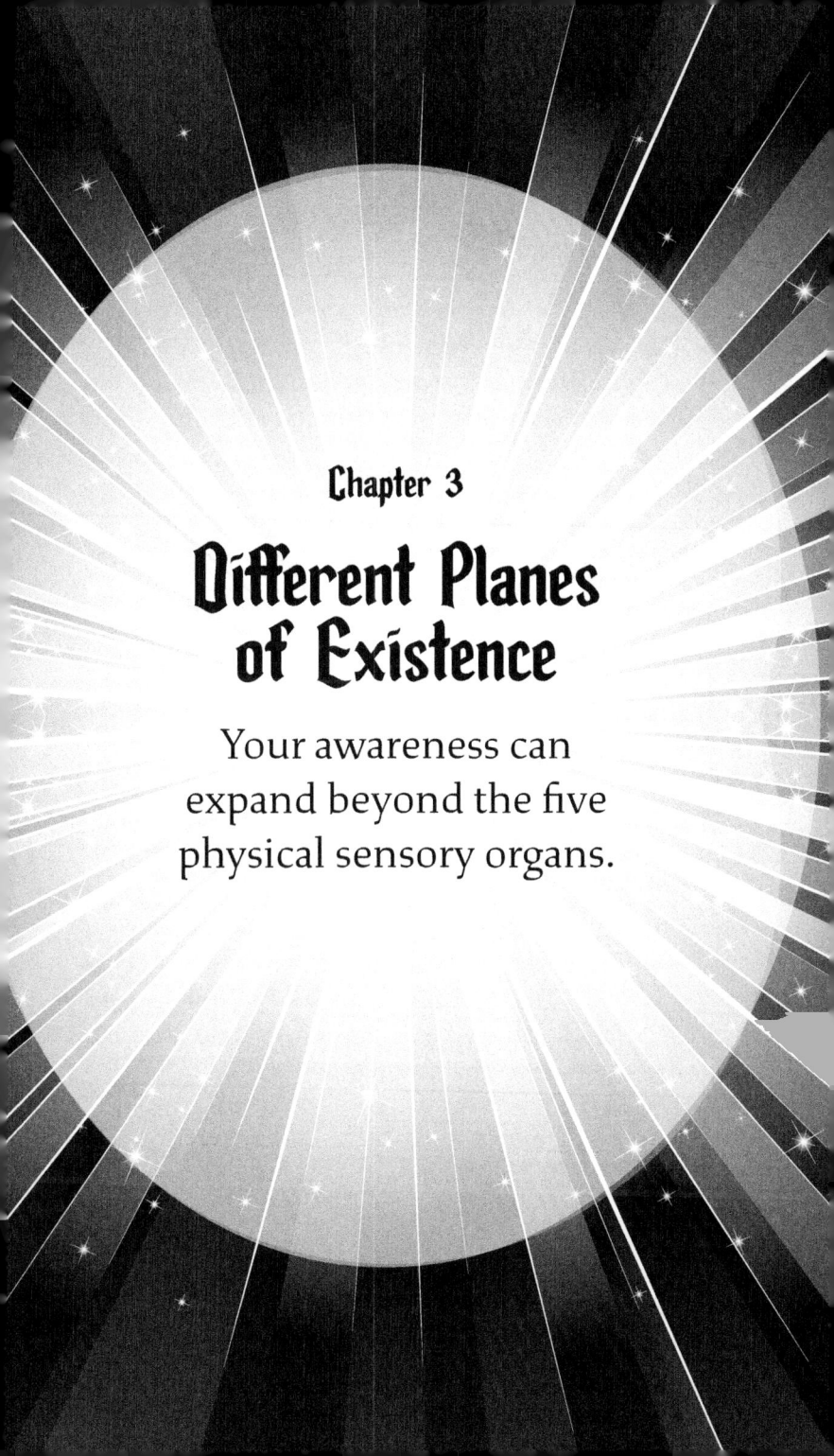

Different Planes of Existence

Your awareness can expand beyond the five physical sensory organs.

Different Planes of Existence

You are spirit experiencing a human body and a mind that gives the illusion that you are separate. Spirit is another word for consciousness and a spiritual experience is just about expanding your awareness. Your awareness can expand beyond the five physical sensory organs. As you are capable of visually perceiving, "within the mind's eye" something on a different plane of existence you are also capable of 'seeing' those on a different plane of existence without the aid of the physical eyes. You are capable of 'hearing' sounds and words on a different plane of existence without the aid of the physical ears. You are capable of perceiving information by a 'feeling' without any outside influences stimulating or triggering it. You are capable of 'smelling' a fragrance or odour that is not in your surroundings. Also, you are capable of being able to perceive something from a different plane of existence through 'taste'.

When connecting with those on a different plane of existence, it is important to have the support and protection of a trusted Spirit Guide to help. You can connect with them by slowing down from your fast-paced life, to become united with their presence. Also, you need to attune your energy to the frequency of love and peace, so that you can effectively connect with them. This means you need to raise your energy level. The higher you can raise your energy level, the easier you will be able to communicate.

Ways to raise your energy level to communicate with the different planes of existence.

—» Listening to positive music
—» To visualise clearing your chakras
—» Using crystals and gemstones
—» Listening to positive music

Listening to positive music - Music has the power to influence how you feel; it can make you cry, or make you feel like you are on top of the world. Music has the power to influence your emotions, so you can use music as a tool to raise your energy level. When depressed, angry or anxious, you can simply listen to high vibrational songs, that will help to elevate your energy. If you want to raise your energy level, it's best to listen to music that is about empowerment, love, and happiness, as this allows communication with your Spirit Guide to be more effective.

To visualise clearing your chakras - Blockages in your chakras are from energies that cause you emotional instability, such as fear, anger, and anxiety. These are negative moods that become stuck within your auric field and emotional body. However, positive moods such as happiness, peace, and joy move in and through your chakras quite naturally keeping them free from blockages. Each chakra is a vortex of energy, it functions as a doorway connecting the energy body in your auric field. If your chakras are free from blockages, the energy flows harmoniously, allowing communication with your Spirit Guide to be more effective.

Using crystals and gemstones - Crystals and gemstones are powerful tools, to help raise your energy level. They are rocks, gems, and stones that come from the planet; the earth energy is grounding and can help protect against negativity. Since ancient times, crystals have been used for their powerful healing properties. Your ancestors intuitively knew that when worn, the energies of the stones would interact with the human electromagnetic field, to bring about energetic changes. There are many crystals and gemstones that can be used to help raise your energy level, so you can effectively communicate with your Spirit Guide; Some of the recommended stones are Clear Quartz, Rose Quartz, Amethyst and Tigers Eye:

Clear Quartz - The seventh chakra stone for the crown of the head is known as the master healer. It amplifies the energy, thoughts, and vibrations of other crystals. It can be used for connecting you with your higher self, intuition, and Guides.

Rose quartz - Activates the heart chakra and promotes positive energy. It enhances all types of love: self-love, love for others, and unconditional love. Raises self-esteem, restores confidence, helps with emotional balance, and releases stress, tension, and anger.

Amethyst - Is a stone of the third eye and crown chakra: It is a super high-vibration crystal that helps you tap into your intuition and connects you to the higher planes of existence.

Tiger's eye - Used for energy amplification and grounding, specifically calming and gets you in a stronger energetic state. If you are an earthy person that vibrates to the energy of the solar plexus, also known as the power chakra; this stone may aid you to bring through a variety of psychic gifts.

Raising your energy will help you maintain a strong connection with your Spirit Guide making it possible and safe to communicate with those on a different plane of existence. Also, when communicating with those on a different plane of existence you have to stay in a state of 'allowing', without letting your thinking mind interfere. This is because you have to try and use all your intuitive senses when different forms of existence come near. You need to feel them, allow the vision of them to appear, and listen to hear what they are communicating. Depending on what your strongest intuitive senses are and what their preferred communication method is, will determine how they communicate with you.

You may hear a voice within your head talking or singing. They may communicate through images, shapes, scenes, or colours within your 'mind's eye'. You may see a shadow out of the corner of your eye. You may feel their emotions or take on physical sensations of how they passed. You may have an idea of what their personality is like.

Ways to practise and improve communication with different planes of existence.

- Attend circles and classes
- Meditate and deal with any personal issues
- Keep a journal of your findings and insights
- Participate in groups online

Attend circles or classes - If you attend circles or classes, it will allow you to practise. Energy can build your ability that will expand and grow over time. Participating in circles or classes can help you develop your ability to communicate much more effectively. This is because you can learn from others and it encourages progress.

Meditate and deal with any personal issues - You need to make yourself a clear channel that is free of any mental or emotional baggage. You need to learn to relax and still the mind. You can do this through daily meditation, to help keep yourself balanced mentally and emotionally. This will help to heighten your senses, recognise your true nature, and alter your consciousness to become aware of those on a different plane of existence.

Keep a journal of your findings and insights - The act of writing allows your subconscious mind to find new ways of improving. You can get insight and write about the things you learn. You can digest information better when writing things down, as you can reflect on your progress. Reflecting on your progress gives you the motivation to advance your ability to communicate better with those on a different plane of existence.

Participate in groups online - You can use online groups to practise communicating with those on a different plane of existence. Online groups include people from all around the world that post photos of their loved ones. This will give you an opportunity to practice, get feedback to boost your confidence and build trust in your ability to connect. When running my online group, I ensured that everyone knew the importance of building a relationship with their Spirit Guide. That they had trust in any feelings, visions, and sensations encountered when making a connection. Also, that knowledge was given to keep grounded and centred.

It is important to keep grounded and centred because over time the build-up of psychic energy can weigh you down. When you ground and keep centred you will feel like you are here in the present. It can help get rid of excess energy, balance your energy, and get you back in touch with your physical body. I like to visualise roots growing from my root chakra into the earth so that unwanted energy moves through the roots down into the ground. I also connect with universal intelligence by imagining a beam of light rising from the top of the head. This is a connection into the spiritual heart of the universe from the crown chakra. A connection to the earth energy and universal intelligence at the same time will keep you centred. Also, it will help you to better connect with those on a different plane of existence.

When you start to connect better you may experience buzzing or ringing in your ears. This is because a different plane of existence is not a separate place, it includes you and exists all around you. You just need to tune in and raise your vibrational frequency to connect. It is like trying to listen to a specific radio station. If the radio station does not have the correct decimal in its frequency, it needs tuning. If the decimal frequency is not correct, you will hear the buzzing or ringing. Hearing this buzzing or ringing is a heightened spiritual awareness.

I started hearing buzzing in my ears before I become Clairaudient, this means hearing those on a different plane of existence. Using this ability, I've passed messages on to others. Also, I have listened to my Spirit Guides whilst going through a spiritual transformation. They have helped me to let go of old toxic patterns and get through a traumatic time in my life.

Activities

Find a quiet place where you feel comfortable to connect with your Spirit Guide. This should be a place where you can tune your energy to the frequency of love and peace. Listen to some positive music, surround yourself with crystals, or visualise clearing and energising your chakras.

Visualise roots growing down into the ground. At the same time visualise a white light rising from the top of your head, connecting to the cosmos. This will allow you to communicate better with your Guide. Also, you need to be in a state of allowing to notice any images, sensations, thoughts, or voices that appear in your mind.

Record any experience you have in a journal; this could be what you hear, see, feel, smell, or taste. If you practice this regularly you will eventually realise your capabilities go beyond the mind and the five physical senses.

Enquire about joining a spiritualist church or centre in your local area. These places can help develop your capabilities. They provide development circles or classes that will allow you to practise. If you do this it will help build trust in your Guide and faith in your ability to communicate. Alternatively, you could use online groups that will give you an opportunity to practise and build trust in your ability to connect.

Chapter 4

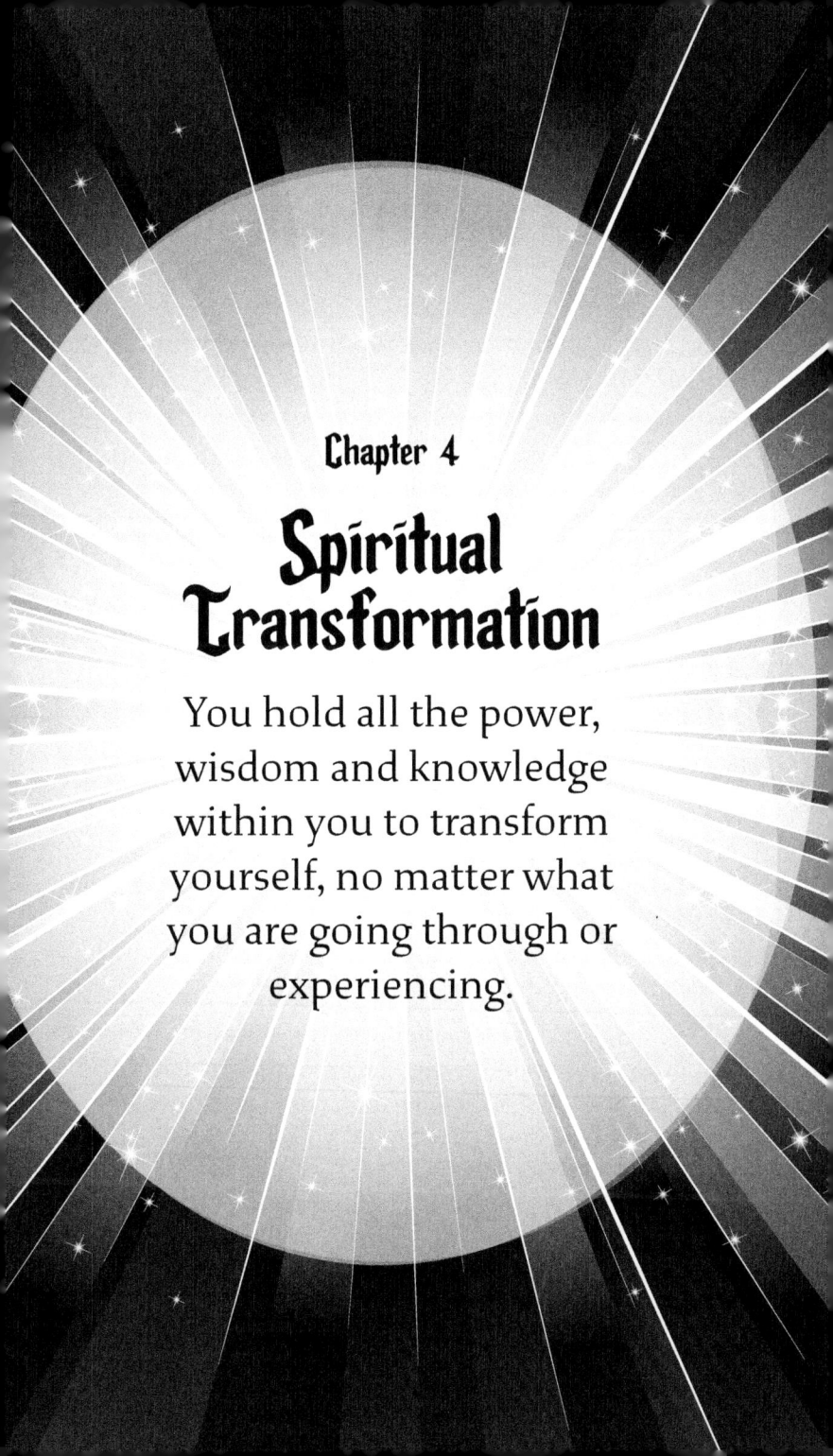

Spiritual Transformation

You hold all the power, wisdom and knowledge within you to transform yourself, no matter what you are going through or experiencing.

Spiritual Transformation

Life is full of experiences that are attracted to you by your higher self for soul expansion, however, your mind might not get it, or think it does not want it. Your mind can lead you to believe that a spiritual transformation is a loss of control or direction. As a result, mistakes or bad choices can be made but this is how you learn. Learning gives you the ability to navigate through the obstacles of life.

You are spirit having a body and mind experience. But the body and mind are just parts of the vessel. The spirit is the navigator. The navigator is always present and aware of the vessel's journey. The journey can be hard and unpredictable. As a result, the vessel can change direction, or it can resist change. When you become aware that you are spirit having a body and mind experience, you will learn to let go and not resist change. You start to change your perception of who you are, including the world around you. You will begin to realise that you have the freedom to create the reality you choose. You also start to find answers because you begin to explore your inner self, which requires a high level of introspection and self-awareness. This awareness is a state of consciousness that can be accessed to promote a greater acceptance of self.

As you discover more about yourself, you will probably find your identity does not match your soul's purpose. There will be a conflict between what you are and who you are expected to be. You will start to slow down and go within. You will start to ask questions and want to explore who you are. You may discover that the person you once were, is no longer you. Also, the life you once had is based on what you thought you needed or what someone else wanted you to be. You may feel as if you are losing your identity. However, it's just your personality's fear of losing control and preventing you from changing into the best version of yourself. Becoming the best version of yourself means to look within yourself through self-monitoring. This means consciously directing your thoughts inward, to become more aware of your inner state of being. Also, observing your thoughts and beliefs to notice what is triggering your emotions. Most of your beliefs are buried in the subconscious and they need to be examined in order to correctly reflect who you really are. You could monitor your inner-self by doing the following:

Allowing yourself some time and space every day – perhaps first thing in the morning or half an hour before sleep, away from the digital distractions and spending some time, reading, writing, meditating, and connecting with the inner-self.

Paying attention to your daily thoughts and being present, so you can observe what's going on inside and around you.

Processing your thoughts through writing, so that you can feel connected and at peace with yourself. This creates more headspace as you let your thoughts flow out onto paper. You could create a journal to record your inner state.

Monitoring your inner self will help grow your understanding of who you are, what your values are, also why you think and act the way you do. It is a form of personal analysis that allows you to bring your life into alignment with your true self. It allows you to reflect upon how you behave and what thoughts enter your mind in response to events in the world around you.

Another way you can monitor your inner self is by **studying your astrological natal chart** as it is a tool for personal growth. It is a powerful 'soul map' that gives you a deeper understanding of yourself. By studying your natal chart, it helps you to understand yourself and how you function in the world around you. It will help you to adapt to changes in the most effective way. It will help you discover more about yourself and your purpose in life.

When studying my natal chart, I started to find transformative cycles by following the planet Pluto. This is the planet of death and rebirth and when it makes a strong transit in your chart, it could be a sign that you are undergoing transformation or that transformation is about to begin. I also discovered that my rising sign is in Scorpio, which is ruled by Pluto. I learned that people with this rising sign have a path of difficult and accelerated soul growth. Every incarnation is important but if you have Scorpio rising, there is something critical about this incarnation that will affect your soul's development. At some point, like a phoenix, I must die and be reborn from my ashes and knowing this has helped me. The Phoenix is the transformational symbol of Scorpio, which means transcending your lower nature into the Phoenix of higher consciousness.

Every person has their unique journey to go through and you have an opportunity for growth. You can all find your rising sign and get familiar with your natal chart. It helps you discover more about yourself as it points out the ways you have been causing your self-fulfilment or self-defeat. Furthermore, if self-defeating behaviours are causing problems for you, you can use the chart as a guide to face them honestly and directly. If you do this, you can tackle those problem areas, realise the most positive potential of every placement and every aspect in your chart.

Studying your natal chart can help you become more self-aware, it gives you a clear perception of your personality, including strengths, weaknesses, thoughts, beliefs, motivations and emotions. Self-awareness allows you to better understand other people, how they perceive you, your attitude and your responses to them in the moment. Self-awareness is achieved through self-inquiry, self-reflection, and self-monitoring. Studying your chart and working with the planetary cycles, can bring you into greater self-awareness and wholeness, and so bring you into balance and harmony with the cosmos. The Hermetic axiom "as above, so below" signifies the belief that the vast mysterious macrocosm of the universe reflects the microcosm of a human being's experience. So, imagine the macrocosm as the universe and the microcosm as being you. You can connect consciously with the same power that drives the entire universe and change how you interact in the world. This means acting as one with the world and not separate to it, which can bring you great inner peace.

On the other hand, a feeling of separation in the world can bring you deep suffering. However, the experience of deep suffering can help you make rapid spiritual progress. This is because suffering gives you a motivation to evolve to higher levels of consciousness that can truly transform your life. Suffering means that you are understanding and learning your life lessons and that you are closer to transcending your current reality. During the process of transcending, you undergo death – the death of the ego. But with every death comes the revival of the phoenix, burning its ashes and rising into a new person.

You hold all the power, wisdom and knowledge within you to transform yourself, no matter what you are going through or experiencing. It is about learning to let go of what you have been conditioned to believe. In addition, letting go of any attachments or feeling of dependency that you have created with regard to your physical health or any other challenges.

Ways to help you get through a spiritual transformation process.

- Meditation
- Prayer
- Attending healing circles
- Interpreting your dreams

Meditation - Meditation can help the body relax and reduces stress. It gives you the ability to direct your thoughts and emotions in a more productive and peaceful direction. It has been demonstrated in the last few years that it has profound self-healing implications for physical and mental health. Meditation is the direct route which takes you into pure awareness in the silent spaces between your thoughts. It helps you become aware of your breathing, any sensations in your body, sounds around you, the sounds within you, your thoughts and emotions. To be aware is to always keep coming back to what is happening now. The 'now' is where you connect with your higher consciousness to witness your thoughts, emotions, actions and the world with non-attachment.

Prayer - Prayer can be an effective method, regardless of your personal religious or spiritual beliefs. It allows areas to be accessed that are beyond the analytical mind, relying on trust. It helps you to believe that transforming yourself is possible and relieves the stress that an illness or injury can cause, especially if the outcome is not certain. It helps you become more attuned to your thoughts, feelings and desires, which in turn brings improved creativity, clarity, energy, and vitality to your entire being.

Healing Circles - Healing circles can help you grow and learn, as it is a group of people bound together by a shared purpose, shared values, and a sense of belonging. Healing circles help you step out of ordinary time into a safe and accepting environment. A healing circle allows you to explore your ways of deepening your capacity to transform and alleviate suffering.

Interpreting your dreams - Understanding your dreams can give you a different perspective on how to tackle life's obstacles. These obstacles can be from deep within or external factors that you may have overlooked. Through understanding your dreams, you can access vital information that is not readily available to you when you are awake. Dreams are formed, in part, by what has gone on the day before. If you understand how the dream is interpreted you can understand something about yourself that you're not consciously aware of during your waking state.

When interpreting dreams, I always take into consideration whether the dreamer experienced it in black and white or in colour. Also, whether the dream was experienced inside or outside, and if it was night or day. Symbolically, this will determine if the person is consciously aware of what is happening in and around them. This would also determine whether the obstacles being faced are internal or external factors that may have been overlooked. I then consider what each symbol represents in the dream; this could be a feeling, a mood, a memory or something from the unconscious. I look closely at the characters, animals, objects, places, emotions, even colour and numbers that are depicted in the dream. Even the most trivial symbol can be significant.

Your dream stories essentially try to strip the emotion out of a certain experience, by creating a memory of it. This mechanism fulfils an important role because when you do not process your emotions, especially negative ones, this increases personal worry and anxiety. Dreams help you find hidden meaning in your subconscious mind; it gives you a chance to become more aware of your inner self and gives you some insight on what needs to be transformed.

Activities

Allow yourself some time and space every day – perhaps first thing in the morning or half an hour before sleep away from any distractions. You can then pay attention to just being present. If your mind starts to wander take notice of your breathing, any sensations in your body, sounds around you and within you, your thoughts and also any emotions. This will allow you to keep coming back to what is happening now.

Record your inner state using a journal. This is a good way to monitor your progress.

Explore the things that make you who you are. You could do this by studying your natal chart, attending meditation classes or healing circles. You could read mindfulness books or keep a journal of your dreams.

Do whatever helps you become more conscious and aware of your inner self to commit to your spiritual transformation. You can do this by monitoring your inner self, which requires a high level of introspection, and that changes the environment around you. Everything is perceived through the self and alters according to your inner state. If you change yourself, your circumstances will change and you can influence and reform your environment with your thoughts and ideas.

Chapter 5

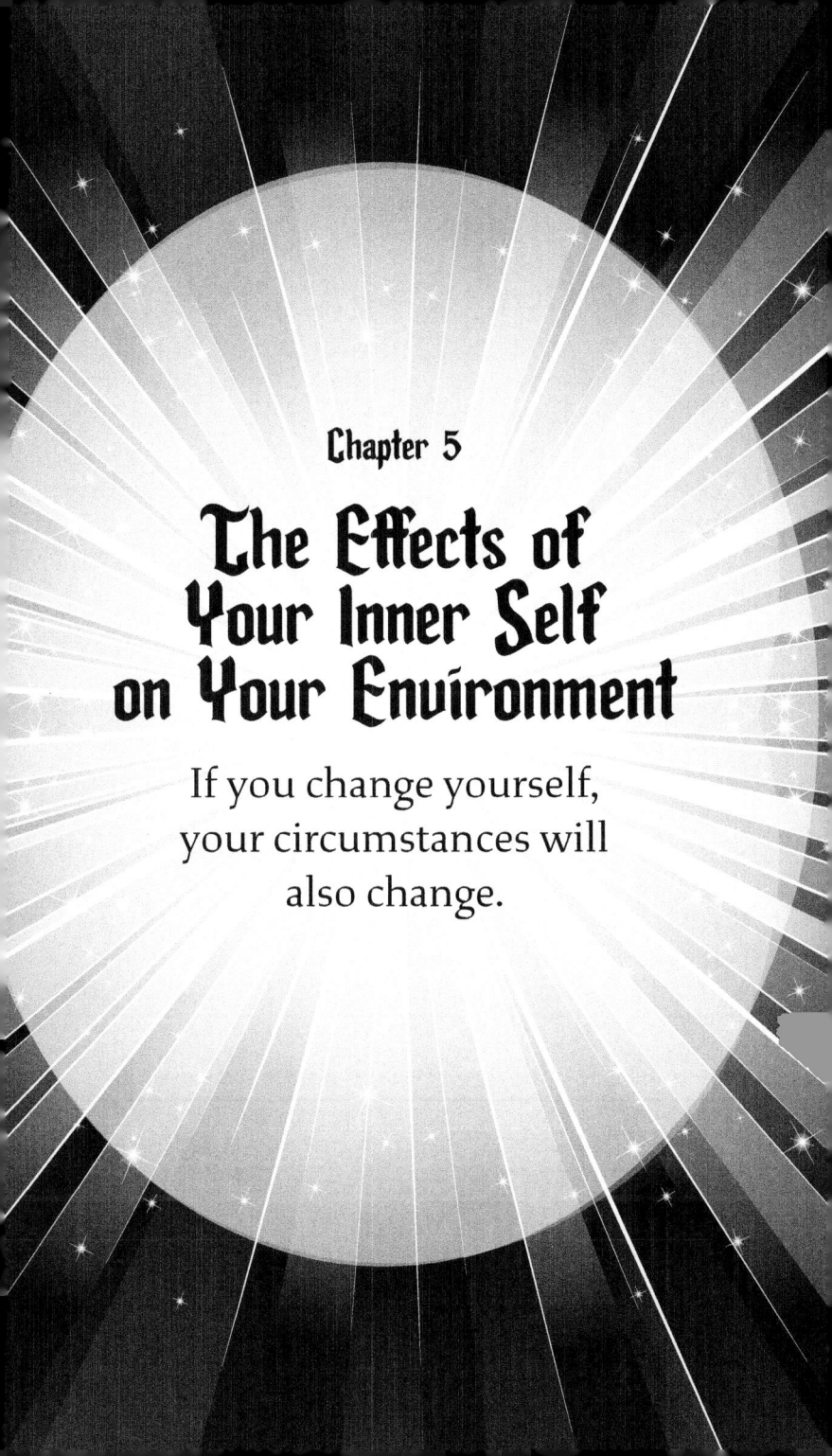

The Effects of Your Inner Self on Your Environment

If you change yourself, your circumstances will also change.

The Effects of Your Inner Self on Your Environment

Throughout your life your identity is being formed through your experiences, relationships, and the world around you. Often, you feel the pressure to define yourself through your job, status, reputation and many other things. The roles you play as a parent, wife/husband, employee, student and so forth is a small part of who you are. You take on these roles based on how you think things should be, or to become the person you think someone else wants you to be. Sometimes you falsely identify yourself with these particular roles, or by someone else's beliefs of who you should be and therefore mistake them for your true authentic self.

Most people are unaware of how much wisdom and power resides in their true authentic self, which is the part of you that is not defined by your job, function or role.

The benefits of knowing your true authentic self are:

—» You are happier and can make better choices about everything because you know yourself better.
—» You understand what motivates you to resist bad habits and develop good ones.
—» You will experience less external conflict because your outside actions are influenced by your inside feelings and values.

The Effects of Your Inner Self on Your Environment

To know your true authentic self might require the letting go of what does not serve you anymore. This could be a relationship or a career that no longer reflects what you truly feel and value.

It is what you feel and value that influences what you experience externally in your environment.

Buddhists believe everything around you including work, family, and relationships is the reflection of your inner self. Everything is perceived through the self and alters according to your inner state. If you change yourself, your circumstances will also change. You can influence and reform your environment through inner change. Your inner state of being is manifested in your surroundings, so when you are full of joy the environment reflects that reality. Likewise, if you are experiencing a distressing internal state, this will be reflected in your surroundings and in how you respond to events in your life.

The main cause of distress to the internal state are limiting beliefs. Your beliefs about yourself shape your reality. For example, I once believed I was unworthy, so that is how I felt. I would reinforce this belief about myself by acting this way. I would disregard anything contrary to my belief and focused on being unworthy. This shaped my reality and how I responded to events in my life. I created my reality with the belief that I was unworthy, and this caused me to suffer in my relationship for many years. My relationship was a direct reflection of my self-worth. It was only when I realised that no-one oversees me and that I am my own authority, that the opinions and demands didn't influence my life anymore. I had been released from the blind pursuit of my illusions, false beliefs, and unnecessary suffering.

Limiting beliefs mainly come from your childhood and your interpretation of the world around you. Limiting beliefs have more of a negative impact on your life than any other factor. However, you can make positive changes to your life by identifying what beliefs are holding you back. Also, by evaluating how your behaviour would change if your limiting beliefs were eliminated from your life. Your life and feelings are a manifestation of your beliefs; if you can change them, your life will change too. It is about completely shifting the way you see yourself and the world around you. Limiting beliefs create false perceptions about yourself that you believe to be true. This is not only reflected in your surroundings, but how people respond to you. Take anyone from your life and look at what they reflect to you. The people you have the deepest connections with are the ones you have chosen to learn and grow with. As you grow your beliefs change and you start to attract new people and situations into your life that reflect your new state of being. This is because when you change yourself you will change your 'mirror'. People in your life that no longer match your mirror will drift away, as you have less in common with them. However, you need to be grateful for all the people that came into your life that have drifted away, for they have helped you change, or improved your life in some way. It does not matter what is going on in your life, you can always find someone to be grateful for.

Gratitude isn't just in your head; it is in your heart and in your senses. So, offering your appreciation is a powerful way to create loving and harmonious connections with others. Appreciation can help you recognise other souls by their unique energy because your heart is open and you attract only love. Deep and harmonious connections based on love goes beyond sharing the same hobbies and opinions: it is an intense magnetic and spiritual bond that you can feel. This could be someone that comes from a different culture, race, or alternative background, but immediately you sense a strong soul connection. These are people in your life that expand your collective growth and evolutionary progress. They will bring in waves of powerful and transformative experiences, not just to help you grow at an individual level, but also a collective level. It is only through this profound experience of relating to another on a soul level that drastic change can occur on both an inner and outer level. Therefore, it's important to find a balance between spending time connecting with the true nature of your being and spending time connecting with others; both these things help you grow your understanding and feeling of interconnectedness. For instance, it's important for me to find love and peace within, so that a harmonious connection with others can be created. This would help grow my understanding and feeling of interconnectedness. In addition, its equally important for me to spend time away from everyday life in self–reflection, to focus intensely on understanding who I am, and what my values are.

Self-reflection allows intense thoughts and feelings to surface, but I let them come and go – without trying to hold onto them, and without trying to push them away. I become aware of them, acknowledge the effect they are having on me, and I try not to judge them. Also, I try not to fight them, but rather be open to what they may have to teach me.

It is your thoughts and feelings that attract situations and people to your life. This is because everything is connected and has an energy field. It is found around every living organism such as, animals, plants and people. This is what sustains life and provides vital energy to all living things. An energy field is generated inside the body and it extends outward to surround it. Like a strong magnet, your field of energy draws other energies to it, and absorbs the power of them. This magnetic energy draws to you the situations, people and events that reinforce whatever you believe and think. It is your thoughts that shape the very essence of you and your life.

Also, there is a life force energy that connects everything that exists and all living beings are taking in this energy at every moment. This energy flows through everything, it is responsive to every thought and emotion. You can use this energy to heal yourself and others. (I explain more about how energy can be used for healing in the next chapter of the book).

Activities

Start to use reflection and introspection to notice more about yourself.

Identify what beliefs are holding you back and evaluate how it affects your life. Start to write a list of things you believe reflect who you are, for example - unworthy, non-confident, unlovable. Also, list how they affect your surroundings and how your respond to events in your life.

Be aware of your thoughts and feelings and let them come and go. You could also write them down, as this will help you acknowledge the effects they are having on you. Try not to judge them, try not to fight them, but be open to what they may have to teach you. You will start to notice more about yourself and the things that previously escaped your notice.

Pay attention to your surroundings and how people respond to you. Start to look at the environment as a reflection of your inner self. When you begin seeing your environment as a reflection of your inner self, you become empowered to solve your problems and create a positive outcome in all situations.

Chapter 6

Energy and How It Can Be Used for Healing

You have a physical body that is a chemical compound of matter that exists and lives with a unique vibrational energy and is also a part of the creation of God.

Energy and How It Can Be Used for Healing

All around you - and throughout the entire universe - circulates a 'life-force' energy. It exists as an energy field around every living thing and circulates through the Earth. The flow of this energy connects everything that exists, and all living beings are taking in this energy at every moment. This energy flows through everything; it is responsive to every thought and emotion. If thoughts are negative, they can easily disrupt your energy field, which means blockages develop. Blockages in your energy field can deplete vitality, leading to ill-health and suffering. However, it is possible to heal and guide others into bringing these blockages to light, so they can be released, by tapping into your clairvoyant and/or clairsentient ability to help find the cause of the problem.

If you have a clairvoyant ability, you can probably 'see' the five layers or energy bodies that comprise the human energy field. These layers are where your mental, physical, spiritual and emotional characteristics are stored. With this ability you can give guidance regarding what is out of balance with other people's energy bodies. If you have clairsentient ability you can tune in, sense and feel other people's emotions. You have a distinct sensitivity to touch, which stems from heightened empathy. Sensitivity to touch is useful to discern areas of the body needing attention and healing. Both clairvoyant and clairsentient abilities can guide and empower others to heal themselves. You can bring blockages to people's attention and guide them using your ability to see or sense where healing is needed.

Also, it is possible to channel healing to others by using this universal life force energy. You can do this by withdrawing from earthly conditions, so that the lower mind is inactive, and your consciousness is switched to a higher level. It means expanding your consciousness and connecting to a collective consciousness. This will allow healing energy to flow through you so that you can channel it to others.

Healing energy can be sent to anyone in the world, and it can take place anywhere at any time. It's your perception of time that keeps your conscious awareness in this physical reality, and that is what limits your ability to manifest change. You probably also experience things as being separate from you, however, this is merely a perception of your limited belief. It's an illusion that time and space are fixed. What is happening here and now, in the present is the most important concept of time. When sending healing, you are moving your consciousness outside the bubble of time and space. There is no past, no future, there is just the 'now'. As you start to expand your consciousness, you start to have a better understanding of how energy works, and you begin to perceive the larger energies in the collective consciousness that you can connect with.

It is possible to channel healing to a body's subtle energy field by expanding consciousness. The body's subtle energy field is a system made up of layers of vibrating energy, each of which have their own specific vibration and purpose. These layers extend outwards from the physical body, with the first layer being closest to the body and the 7th layer being furthest away from the body. Each layer also increases in vibration as it moves outwards, with the 7th layer carrying the highest vibration. Also, there are seven energy centres or chakras that are connected. Each chakra is a vortex of energy and functions as a doorway, connecting the energy bodies in your auric field. This allows higher frequencies to flow through to the physical body. A chakra is a centre of activity that receives and expresses life force energy. You hold every thought, emotion and feeling in one of your seven chakras and they may become blocked and need to be released.

Each chakra connected to the auric field has a colour that vibrates and resonates, and these colours are red, orange, yellow, green, blue, indigo and violet. The seven layers of the auric field and chakras are:

Etheric Layer - A layer of energy that is associated with the physical body. It is connected to the Root chakra, which is the colour red. It represents your foundation and feeling of being grounded. The Root chakra is located at the base of spine in the tailbone area. It governs your emotions around love, sex, self-expression, desire and survival issues such as financial independence, money and food. It's associated with the reproductive glands, controls sexual development and hormones. It influences the reproductive organs, kidney and spine.

Emotional Layer - A layer of energy that regulates the emotional state and where your feelings reside. It is connected to the Sacral chakra, which is the colour orange. This chakra is associated with your connection and ability to accept others and accept new experiences. It is located at the lower abdomen, about two inches below the navel and two inches in. It governs your sensuality, your creativity, your self-esteem and your sense of abundance, well-being, and pleasure. It is associated with the adrenal glands and regulates the immune system and metabolism. It influences organs like the bladder, prostate, ovaries, kidneys, gall bladder, bowel and spleen.

Mental Layer - A layer of energy where you process ideas, thoughts, and beliefs. This is the conscious mind, logic, active thinking, and intellect. It represents thoughts, cognitive processes and state of mind. This is connected to the Solar Plexus chakra and its colour is yellow. It is associated with your ability to be confident and in control of your lives. It is located at the upper abdomen in the stomach area. It governs your self-worth, self-esteem, self-confidence, your fears, the triggers that cause them and your anxiety. It is associated with the pancreas and regulates your metabolism. It influences organs such as the intestines, pancreas, liver, bladder, stomach, and upper spine.

Astral Layer - This layer is the bridge between the physical planes and the spiritual realm. It is connected to the Heart chakra and is the colour green. It is also associated with your ability to love. It is located at the centre of the chest just above the heart. It governs your emotions around guilt, abundance, love, joy and inner peace. It is associated with the thymus gland; regulates the immune system and also influences organs such as the heart and lungs.

Etheric Template - A nexus between the physical and spiritual realms. Free of time and space it represents the entire blueprint of the body that exists on this physical plane. It includes everything you create on this physical level including your identity, personality, and overall energy. It is connected to the throat chakra and the colour blue and your ability to communicate. It governs your emotions around communication, self-expression and the truth. It is associated with the thyroid gland and regulates body temperature and metabolism. It influences organs such as the bronchial tubes, vocal cords, and respiratory system.

Celestial field - Represents the connection to the Divine and all other beings where unconditional love and feelings of oneness flow. It is connected to the third eye chakra. The colour indigo is associated with your third eye chakra, which is also connected to your ability to focus on and see the big picture. It is located at the forehead between the eyes. It governs your intuition, psychic abilities, imagination and wisdom plus the ability to think and make decisions. It is associated with the pituitary gland; produces hormones and it influences organs such as the eyes, pineal glands and brain.

Kether Template - Represents the feeling of being one with the Universe. It holds all the information about your soul and previous lifetimes. It is connected to the Crown chakra and is associated with the colour violet and located at the very top of the head. It governs your connection to yourself, your bliss, and your inner and outer beauty. It is associated with the pineal gland; regulates biological cycles, including sleep. It also influences organs such as the spinal cord and brain stem.

Each chakra vibrates at a different frequency, and it generates the colour within the light spectrum. Light itself is a vibration, a wave that is measured by length and frequency. As all light waves move at the same speed, the number of wave crests passing by in a given time period varies on the length. A long wavelength has a low frequency, whereas a short wavelength has a high frequency. The light reflected from an object and which you recognise as colour is a mixture of light at various wavelengths within the visible region of the spectrum. The light in the region with the longest wavelengths are seen as red, and the light in the region with the shortest wavelengths is seen as violet. Red light is at the bottom, whereas violet light is at the top of the spectrum. Violet is the colour resonating with the Crown chakra, the chakra that connects you with the Divine. (The Crown chakra further resonates with white, which is not a colour itself but absent of all colours). In other words, the higher the chakra the higher it's inherent frequency. The more you develop all your chakras the higher you will ultimately raise your overall frequency.

Scientists have discovered that your DNA emits a certain level of light and believe that the body's biofeedback system depends on light waves. Light is responsible for the photo-repair of body cells and when you are ill, your light waves are out of sync.

A light wave is a type of electromagnetic wave. All waves really are essentially travelling energy and the more energy in a wave, the higher its frequency. The lower the frequency the less energy in the wave, so you vibrate energetically at a particular frequency. The lower the frequency the denser your energy and the heavier your problems seem. The higher the frequency of your energy or vibration, the lighter you feel in your physical, emotional, and mental body. It means you experience greater personal power, clarity, peace, love and joy and you have little, if any, discomfort or pain in your physical body and your emotions are easily dealt with. Your energy is literally full of light! Your life flows with synchronicity and you manifest what you desire with ease. Overall, your life takes on a very positive quality.

To help raise your vibration you can use 'solfeggio frequencies', which are reputed to be the original frequencies used by the Gregorian Monks when they chanted. The chant, based on just six notes, penetrates deep into the conscious and subconscious mind, drawing forth emotional reactions which you are sometimes unable to completely control. Each frequency of the 6-tone scale is believed to balance the whole body, the physical, spiritual and emotional. The notes in the scale are:

—» "UT" – which cycles at 396 Hz (aids in the liberation of fear and guilt).
—» "RE" – which cycles at 417 Hz (helps facilitates change and undo situations).
—» "MI" – which cycles at 528 Hz (aids in transformation and miracles like DNA repair).

—» "FA" – which cycles at 639 Hz (helps you to connect/aids in relationships).
—» "SOL" – which cycles at 741 Hz (it awakens intuition).
—» "LA" – which cycles at 852 Hz (helps you to return to spiritual order).

The Solfeggio frequencies are linked to mathematics and religion. It is said to have a powerful impact on one's state of mind and health. The basic principle of Solfeggio frequency healing is that of resonance – the idea that every object is in a state of vibration and therefore creates a frequency. When you are in resonance, you are in balance because every cell in your body absorbs and emits sound with a particular optimum resonate frequency.

For example, the frequency of 432 Hz and 528 Hz tunes create resonance in your physical, mental, emotional and spiritual body. Music with a frequency of 432 Hz and of 528 Hz are both chords of the same perfect melody of the universe. You can use them in healing work. I listen to both 432 Hz and 528 Hz tunes to resonate with the divine energy every day. I encourage you to try and listen to both 432 Hz and 528 Hz sounds to feel the difference in your heart. According to Dr Leonard Horowitz, 528 Hz is a frequency that is central to the "musical mathematical matrix of creation." He calls it the 'love frequency' and claims that it resonates at the heart of everything and "connects one's heart and spiritual essence to the spiralling reality of heaven and Earth".

Most of the ancient Egyptian and Greek instruments were tuned to play music with a frequency of 432 Hz as well as Tibetan 'singing bowls'.

Music based on 432 Hz is said to transmit beneficial healing energy, because it is a mathematical 'pure tone' fundamental to nature. Playing music tuned to 432 Hz will fill you with a sense of peace and wellbeing; it will resonate inside of your body, release emotional blockages, take you into a natural relaxation state and expand your consciousness. This sound vibration can engage your energy field and physical body in a state of resonance with the earth's natural electromagnetic field. It activates, opens, balances and heals your heart chakra. This frequency encourages you to restore human consciousness to its full power and potential.

In addition, sound with 528 Hz resonates at the heart of the Sun (recorded by NASA scientists). Sunbeams, the rainbow, flowers, grass and even the buzzing of bees vibrates at 528 Hz. Nature in balance vibrates at 528 Hz. It is the frequency of life itself.

Your body's vibration can move out of its base resonance frequency very easily when you experience any type of stress, and the body then becomes out of balance.

Using sound vibration can make you feel more balanced, so can using crystals as they have healing properties that can transmit subtle electromagnetic energy. They also have the capacity to absorb, reflect and radiate light in the form of intelligent fields of stable energy that increase the flow of universal life force energy within your physical and subtle body. Crystals are also able to take energy that is out of balance and put it back into its natural balanced state. They help you connect to the Earth when you wear them close to your skin or place them in your environment. Furthermore, with every thought and intention crystals pick up on your unique vibrational energy; they amplify the positive vibes that you're cultivating and help you on your spiritual journey. They work to hold your intention and remind you of your connection to the universal life force energy that flows through everything.

Everything is energy. The universe is a creation of God from which everything originates. It is an energy flow with an infinite number of vibrations. Everything that lives and exists has its own unique vibration that is only a tiny part of that infinite energy flow. It includes the material universe; life in all its forms, energy, matter, and everything you can perceive with your senses. This means you have a physical body that is a chemical compound of matter that exists and lives with a unique vibrational energy and is also a part of the creation of God.

Activities

Start to notice your surroundings and how you see or feel around other people. You might have clairvoyant and/or clairsentient abilities.

—» If you have a clairsentient ability you will have a heightened sense of empathy, be very sensitive to people, and have a strong gut feeling.

—» If you have clairvoyant abilities, you will have a clear vision, be very receptive to other people and able to see auras (colours surrounding other people).

—» It is possible to have a mixture of clairsentient and/or clairvoyant abilities, which can be used to guide and heal others, so it is worth learning to develop them.

Here are some ways you can help develop your clairvoyant or clairsentient abilities:

—» Meditate every day for at least 10 – 15 minutes, to keep in a relaxed state and raise your energetic vibration.

—» Practice psychometry by connecting to objects that are closely connected with other people to pick up information about their character, surrounding, and events connected with them. You can use personal items like jewellery, such as watches or necklaces. At first, visions may just be flashes of images, shapes and colours but this a psychic skill can be developed overtime.

—» Use visualisation exercises to help develop your psychic abilities, specifically, clairvoyance.

—» Read relevant books.

—» Practice learning to see auras.

—» Keep a journal.

—» Join a spiritual development circle or take a class.

Take time to withdraw from earthly conditions, so that the lower mind becomes more inactive, and your consciousness is switched to a higher level. The universe has a consciousness, a universal energy that you can use to channel to others. You can become a conduit for universal energy to flow through. If you want to learn more about this you could go on an Angelic healing, Crystal healing, or Reiki healing course.

Listen to music with a frequency of 432 Hz, and love meditations with a frequency of 528 Hz as they are both chords of the same perfect melody of the universe, which you can use in healing work. Listening to music or chants linked to solfeggio frequencies will have a powerful impact on your state of mind and health.

Surround yourself with crystals as they have healing properties that can transmit subtle electromagnetic energy. They also have the capacity to absorb, reflect and radiate light in the form of intelligent fields of stable energy that increase the flow of universal life force energy within your physical and subtle body.

Chapter 7

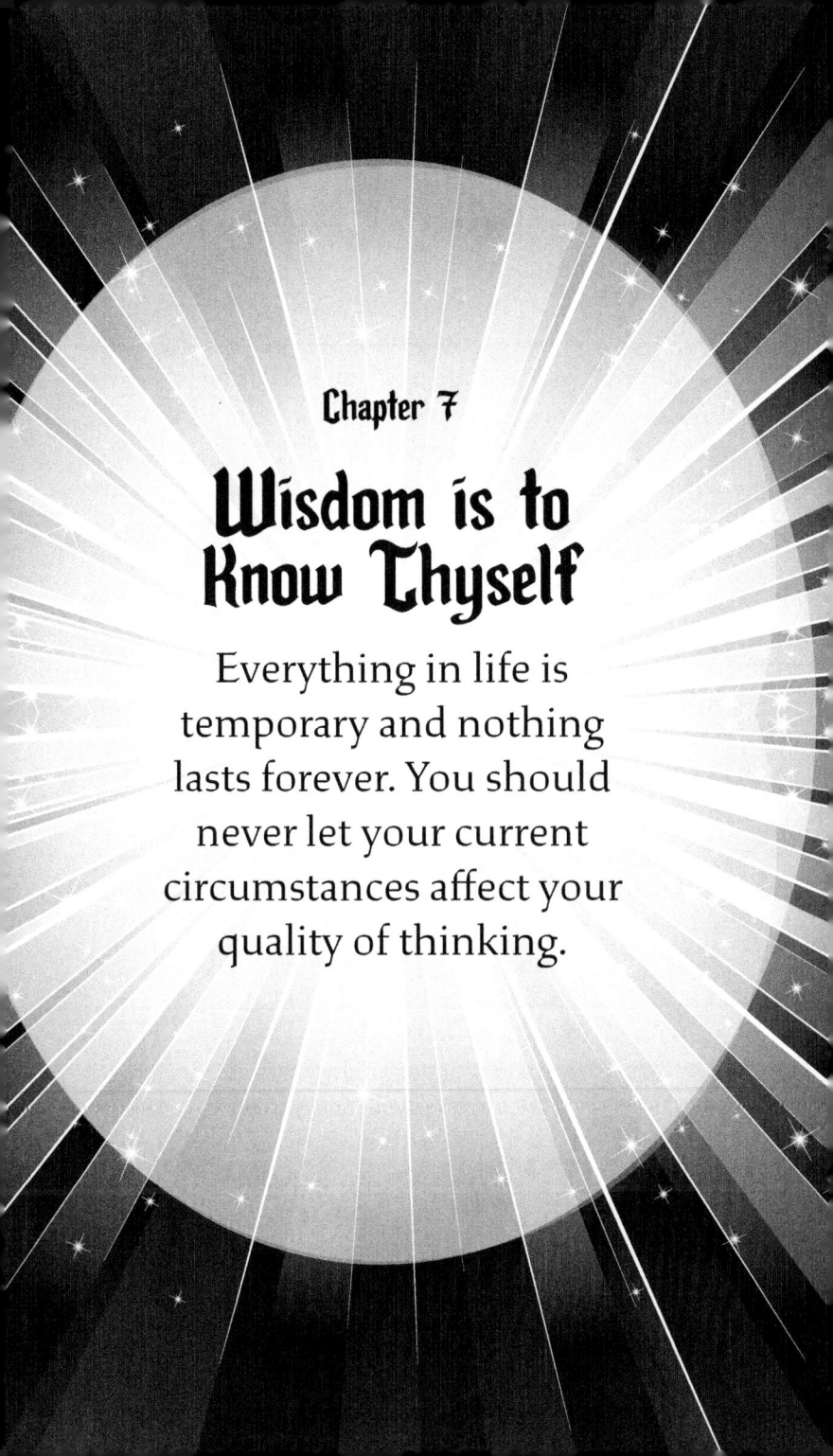

Wisdom is to Know Thyself

Everything in life is temporary and nothing lasts forever. You should never let your current circumstances affect your quality of thinking.

Wisdom is to Know Thyself

You have a physical body that is a chemical compound of matter that is self-perpetuating and self-correcting, just like the external universe. There are billions of cells in your body which all function on their own. Yet at the same time, they are also all connected to each other and form one whole and this is the same in the cosmos. That which exists in the external universe appears in the internal cosmos of the human body. It is made from the same things that is found among the stars in space. According to Scientist Carl Sagan, "You are star stuff, from the nitrogadsyen in your DNA, the calcium in your teeth, and the iron in your blood. The six most common elements of life on Earth (including more than 97 percent of the mass of a human body) are carbon, hydrogen, nitrogen, oxygen, sulphur, and phosphorus. Those same elements are abundant at the centre of the Milky Way galaxy. The Cosmos is within you. You are made of star-stuff. You are a way for the universe to know itself".

You also need to 'know thyself' in order to know the universe. Aristotle said, "To know thyself is the beginning of wisdom." And, according to Socrates, the path to such self-knowledge is through inner reflection, or what is now call 'introspection'.

The path to self - knowledge is a realisation of your true mind that is all knowing, all powerful, and all creative. Your mind is part of the one Universal Mind. The Universal Mind is Omniscience (all knowing),

Omnipotence (all powerful) and Omnificence (all creative).

You have access to all knowledge, known and unknown; you have access to an infinite power for which nothing is impossible; you have access to the limitless creativity of the One Creator. All these attributes are present within you at all times in their potential form. You are made of the same heavenly energies of that which is above. Every cell in your organism corresponds with the 'cell' in the divine organism or the universe. Helena Petrovna Blavatsky a Russian occultist, philosopher, and author who co-founded the 'Theosophical Society' in 1875, wrote: "As in the Microcosm (Man), so in the Macrocosm (Universe), every 'organ' in it is a sentient entity, and every particle of matter or substance, from the physical molecule up to the spiritual atom, is a cell, a nerve centre, which communicates with the brain-stuff or that substance on the plane of divine thought in which the prime ideation is produced. Therefore, man is produced in the image of God - or Divine nature. Every cell in the human organism mysteriously corresponds with a 'cell' in the divine organism of the manifested universe".

That which exists in the external universe (Macrocosm) also appears in the internal cosmos (Microcosm). There is no separation between you and the universe. The same forces that keep the atoms in your body and your environment in constant motion, keep the planets in motion. The planetary movement in motion influence moments in time. Since there is no separation between you and the universe, your moment of birth recorded on the celestial clock is important. The planets continue to move, engaging with the fixed-in-time energies of your astrological birth chart, which means every event and development down here has its correspondence in the sky. The position of the sun, stars, moon and planets at the time of your birth is said to shape your personality, affect your romantic relationships and predict your economic fortunes, among other divinations – "as above so below".

"As above, so below", can also be "as within, so without", which means your outer world is nothing more than a reflection of your inner world. What you think about is reflected in the world you live. If you think positive, positivity will follow; if you think negative, negativity will follow. Whatever you think consciously will manifest in your life because your attitude, belief and emotions create your reality. Both the inner and outer world correspond, just as there is a sacred connection between us and God or the Divine

'As above, so below', 'as within, so without', can also be expressed as 'as the universe, so the soul'.

The human soul is made of the matter that has always existed in the spiritual universe.

The Earth is a mere image of the realities of the spiritual world and exists only as the nursery for the individualisation of the soul. The human soul is a creation of God and not an emanation or projection from God. It was created in the image and likeness of its Creator (Genesis 1:27), though not of the Creator's essence or substance, but of the matter that already existed as part of the spiritual universe. The creation of the human soul took place long before the appearance of mortals in the flesh. Prior to their appearance, the soul had its existence in the spirit world as a substantial conscious entity without visible form or individuality, but with a distinct personality. Every soul was different from all others and had a consciousness of its existence, and an awareness of a relationship to its Creator.

Although, each soul is different everything that consists in the universe is made up of energy and has its own vibrational frequency. Things appear separate and solid but every atom and molecule vibrates at a certain motion, speed and frequency. Science through quantum physics is showing us that everything in the universe is energy. At a sub-atomic level, you don't find matter, but only pure energy and vibration. Everything is made up of energy at different vibration levels to form the matter around you.

This means your thoughts can emit a unique energy and vibration that form your experience around you.

It's been proven by scientists that energy is never created or destroyed, so when you think a thought, you are emitting energy that is a unique electro-magnetic unit going into the universe. Your thoughts are like cosmic waves penetrating time and space, so you need to be aware of what you think about. Thoughts travel in waves, just as wireless waves travel, and they attract thoughts and ideas from the minds of others that can assist in the manifesting of your desires. This is because it is only you that is responsible for your frequency of vibration by what you think about. If you think about what you want it's a desire flowing from a positive frequency. However, if you think about what you don't yet have, it's a fear vibrating at a negative frequency, therefore, it's important to be conscious of your frequency by focusing on the feeling of what you want to experience.

You could start to do this by looking for the good in every bad situation and realising that negative circumstances exist to help you to create positive circumstances. This is because it's important you find the stability within yourself and in everything you do. This requires a lot of soul searching and understanding of your thoughts, beliefs and actions that help pinpoint areas that need to be balanced. So, every time you allow yourself to feel an extreme emotion, you create the equal experience of the opposite. When you acknowledge that one-sidedness is merely an illusion, and not actual truth, it opens the doorway to seeing the rest of world for what it truly is. This is a completely balanced system that is fully equilibrated because of the divine order that exists. As you allow yourself to perceive both sides simultaneously (the whole, positive and negative) you open yourself to the divine perfection of the universe.

How you feel is constantly changing because it's human nature. You are affected by how your mood swings, so, it is important to find a balance. This can be done by lessening the effect of the negativity in your life, by overcoming negativity and remaining positive.

There are times when things are out of rhythm and it can make you feel uncomfortable. You need to stay focused on your vision and go with the flow instead of resisting it. If you are experiencing hard times you need to understand that good times will come. Everything in life is temporary and nothing lasts forever. You should never let your current circumstances affect your quality of thinking. You should always look with positive expectation to the future.

It is important not to get attached and base your happiness on external objects, people, or circumstances that lie outside of your control. You should instead strive towards a state of consciousness that is indifferent, blissful and non-attached, despite the conditions you may find yourself in. You can get attached to things outside of your control based on fear and insecurity because the need for security is based on not knowing the true Self. When you are secure in the moment, the dependence on the physical or material is detached and there is freedom.

You can make things happen by letting the universe conspire events in your favour. It doesn't mean not taking action and simply leaving it up to the universe, it means being flexible and not clinging to any idea of how it should all turn out. When you do that, your intentions become your reality. However, every action has consequences and will produce specific results in your life. Life is like a game of chess. Every move is a choice, that choice is the cause and, that cause has an effect. Allan Rufus, said, "Life is like a game of chess. To win, you have to make a move. Knowing which move to make comes with IN-SIGHT and knowledge, and by learning the lessons that are accolated along the way. You become each piece within the game called life!" Absolutely every action you take and every thought, has its corresponding effect, whether it is instant or in the future. You need to become aware of the fact that you can alter your reality by simply changing your thoughts. The power of your thoughts, desires and words determines your reality. So, thinking positive thoughts and keeping a high-vibrational state should be a very important aspect of your daily life.

You can also change your reaction, as well as your thoughts, by altering your perception and understanding. These changes will help you develop enough wisdom to know that your actions can lead to happiness and freedom or to further suffering. When you develop wisdom, you will realise that you are a conscious creator, and that the universe is ever listening and responding to you.

You have the power to consciously create anything in your spiritual or higher energetic state. This is because you are purely a sentient being with energies that are genderless in nature. The masculine and feminine is simply a dualistic function associated with the physical universe that has been designed to reproduce.

To know you are genderless in nature is to understand oneness and that there are higher states of consciousness.

Activities

Examine your life and see where you can find a connection with the world surrounding you. Also, start to become aware of your thinking habits and what they create in your external life. If you do this, you will realise that you are consciousness with a mind having a human existence. Also, a physical body that is a chemical compound of matter that is self-perpetuating and self-correcting just like the external universe.

Discover more about yourself. Who are you? What it is you do? And how does it impact your life? Follow the path to self-knowledge through inner reflection or what is now termed introspection.

Study your astrological natal chart because your personal energy field or microcosm map reflects and remains connected to the energy patterns within the solar system. The position of the sun, stars, moon and planets at the time of your birth is said to shape your personality, affect your romantic relationships and predict your economic fortunes, among other divinations – 'as above so below'.

Begin to understand that you are an integral part of the universe. There can be no you without the universe, and no universe without you. This is because your soul is created in the image and likeness of its Creator.

Start to become conscious of your vibrational frequency by focusing on the feeling of what you want to experience. For instance, if you think about what you want it will be a desire flowing from a positive frequency. Whereas, if you think about what you don't yet have, it's a fear vibrating at a negative frequency. Your thoughts can materialise regardless of whether they are positive or negative. You can avoid negative thoughts by filling your life with the music, people, smells, sights, materials and activities that bring you joy - as this will automatically raise your vibrational frequency.

Start to focus on the feeling of what you want to experience by looking for the 'good' in every bad situation and realising that negative circumstances exist to help you create positive circumstances. Look for the good in every bad situation, try not to get attached and base your happiness on external objects, people, or circumstances that lie outside of your control.

Start to believe you have the power to consciously create anything in your spiritual or higher energetic state, because you are purely a sentient being with an energy that is genderless in nature.

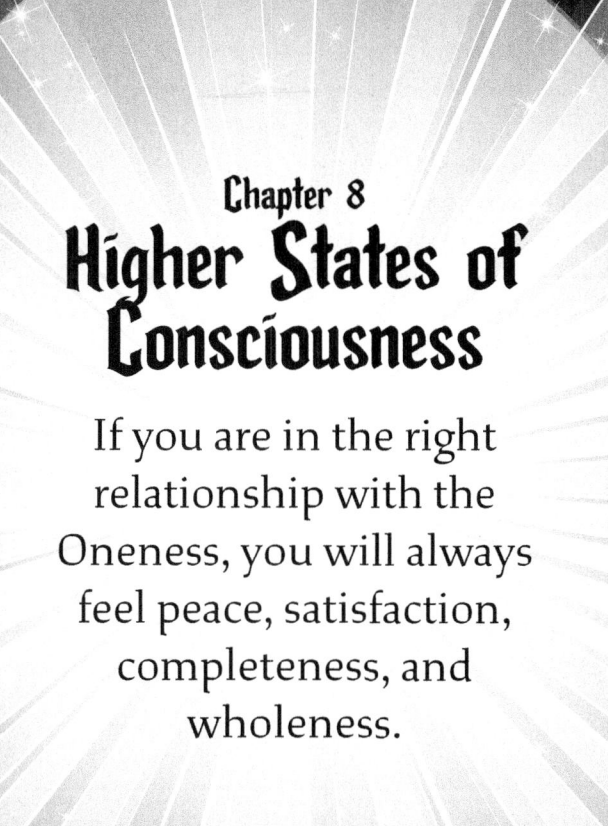

Chapter 8
Higher States of Consciousness

If you are in the right relationship with the Oneness, you will always feel peace, satisfaction, completeness, and wholeness.

Higher States of Consciousness

Your physical body and mind are forever changing but awareness is always there in the background. It is your changeless and formless self and it's the stillness of your mind. It's also the observer experiencing and remaining consciously aware of whatever passes before you. Think about clouds passing by in the sky as being your thoughts constantly changing, and the sky being the stillness of your mind, or your changeless and formless self.

Whatever your limited mind perceives as the sky is but an illusion, because beyond the sky is the cosmos that is limitless.

What might seem impossible, considering physical limitations in the physical world, is actually fully accessible, by expanding your awareness to a higher state of consciousness. Higher states of consciousness can be obtained through the practice of yoga, meditation, or prayer. The higher states of consciousness are:

— » Unity consciousness
— » Transcendental consciousness
— » Cosmic consciousness
— » God consciousness

Unity consciousness - 'Unity Consciousness' is the realisation that separation and duality is an illusion. When you attain unity consciousness you begin to see through this illusion. This is where you find the true centre of your being. This is where you are connected directly to the Oneness. This is where you can access infinite wisdom and infinite knowledge. If you are in the right relationship with the Oneness, you will always feel peace, satisfaction, completeness, and wholeness. You will start to truly love yourself, in addition to seeing the spark and miracle in every being. Maharishi Mahesh Yogi said, "only in unity consciousness is the gap between inner and outer reality, between subjective and objective existence fully bridged". As proclaimed in the Bhagavad Gita, "in the highest state of enlightenment, one sees the Self in all beings, and all beings in the Self".

When you attain unity consciousness you start to care enough to want to make changes through your actions. You must therefore learn to direct your heart and mind enough to develop the knowledge to act with care. This means thinking and ultimately acting in ways that unite you to yourself and to others.

Transcendental Consciousness - This is a state where the mind and the senses are completely silent, but awareness is fully awake. This level of awareness has the quality of bliss which can be reached through the practise of meditation. It is pure self-awareness, and with regular practice leads to higher states of consciousness.

Maharishi Mahesh Yogi said, "Transcendence is the state where the mind has moved beyond everything other than itself. That means it has transcended all kinds of activity, small and big, and it has settled down in its own authority, in its own sovereignty, into the unbounded dignity of its own intelligence. And in this state, transcendental consciousness turns out to be a lively field of all possibilities". Transcendental

Consciousness is blissful awareness, a balanced state of fulfilment beyond change, time, and space. It is the experience of one's innermost self which is pure consciousness. Transcendental consciousness is not just a state of relaxation, but an altered state of awareness. It is an inner awareness of consciousness, rather than of an outer awareness of a conscious experience.

Cosmic Consciousness - Richard Maurice Bucke is a Canadian psychiatrist that wrote about three levels of consciousness found in all living beings. The first level is simple awareness that both mankind and animals possess; the second level is self-awareness, which includes thought, reason, imagination and the awareness which mankind possesses. The third is 'cosmic consciousness' which is a higher and more spiritual awareness than most ordinary people possess. Cosmic consciousness includes a spiritual understanding and awareness of eternal life and that 'God' is actually the whole universe.

Cosmic consciousness is a realisation that you are not only mind and matter but all of existence, including the physical universe. Cosmic consciousness is beyond that of self-awareness, it is knowledge instead of mere belief. It's a recognition of oneness and unity with the universe.

Dr. Peter Fenwick, a highly regarded neuropsychiatrist who has been studying the human brain, consciousness, and the phenomenon of near-death experience (NDE) for 50 years has undertaken some extensive research which suggests that consciousness persists after death.

He believes the mind filters and perceives only a tiny part of the cosmos's intrinsic 'consciousness'.

According to Fenwick, our mind tricks us into perceiving a false duality of self and others when in fact there is only unity. You are not separate from other aspects of the universe but an integral and inextricable part of it.

God-Consciousness - This is where wisdom and knowledge can be gained through the result of learning about your true inner guidance. Dr Paul Leon Master's teachings explain that you need to activate the 'God power' within you. This is to allow God's will to be totally in charge of your life and to surrender your body, mind, and soul, so that you can be used in God's presence. God is the life-force and reality in everything.

When you start to connect with the essence of life and experience God consciousness, things begin to become clearer to you. It is a connection within that creates the capacity to see and understand things more deeply. So, to reach this level of consciousness you need to be aware of God as you are yourself. For instance, I started connecting with Lord Shiva, which created the capacity for me to see more deeply. This is because connecting with Shiva removes your ignorance, your false sense of duality and your sense of separation. I started to see everything as a blessing and an expression of love. Also, I started to accept my imperfections and embrace my own identity.

This kind of inner work requires a courageous commitment to self-forgiveness and self-love.

At this level of consciousness, you can find joy in everything and see beauty in all that you encounter. You can feel so connected and in tune with life, finding joy in the simplest things. You become aware of yourself and the world around you and it is a unique and subjective experience. Master [Sri Ramana], said that his experience was 'already here'. When you love God, you think he is an object. But he is the subject. So, you have to learn to surrender to the subject. The ego is the object. You merge into the subject so that no object is left behind.

Activities

Practice daily consciousness meditation, repeat affirmations and becoming intimately acquainted with the power of 'conscious breathing'.

Start to become more aware of your surroundings. Try to focus on every sound such as birds or other animals in the background. As your mind becomes aware of its surroundings, begin to sense a feeling of connectedness with the world around you.

Practice mindfulness by letting go of disturbing notions and thoughts. Allow your mind to easily settle inward, until you experience the most silent and peaceful level of your own awareness.

Start to focus, concentrate, and bring your attention to your energy centres, known as chakras. This is important for spiritual awakening. Each energy centre is important for its own reasons and balancing them will help you with understanding the inner awareness of consciousness, which is a state of fulfilment beyond change, time, and space.

Practice yoga, meditation, prayer, and acts of faith. This will allow your mind to be elevated beyond the awareness of the self and the ego and enter a place of oneness and unity with the universe.

Use self-reflection to come to know the Creator within, recognise the power, truth, and radiance you hold within you.

Accept your imperfections and embrace your identity. Do some inner work that requires a courageous commitment to self-forgiveness and self-love. Start to see everything as a blessing and an expression of love.

Chapter 9

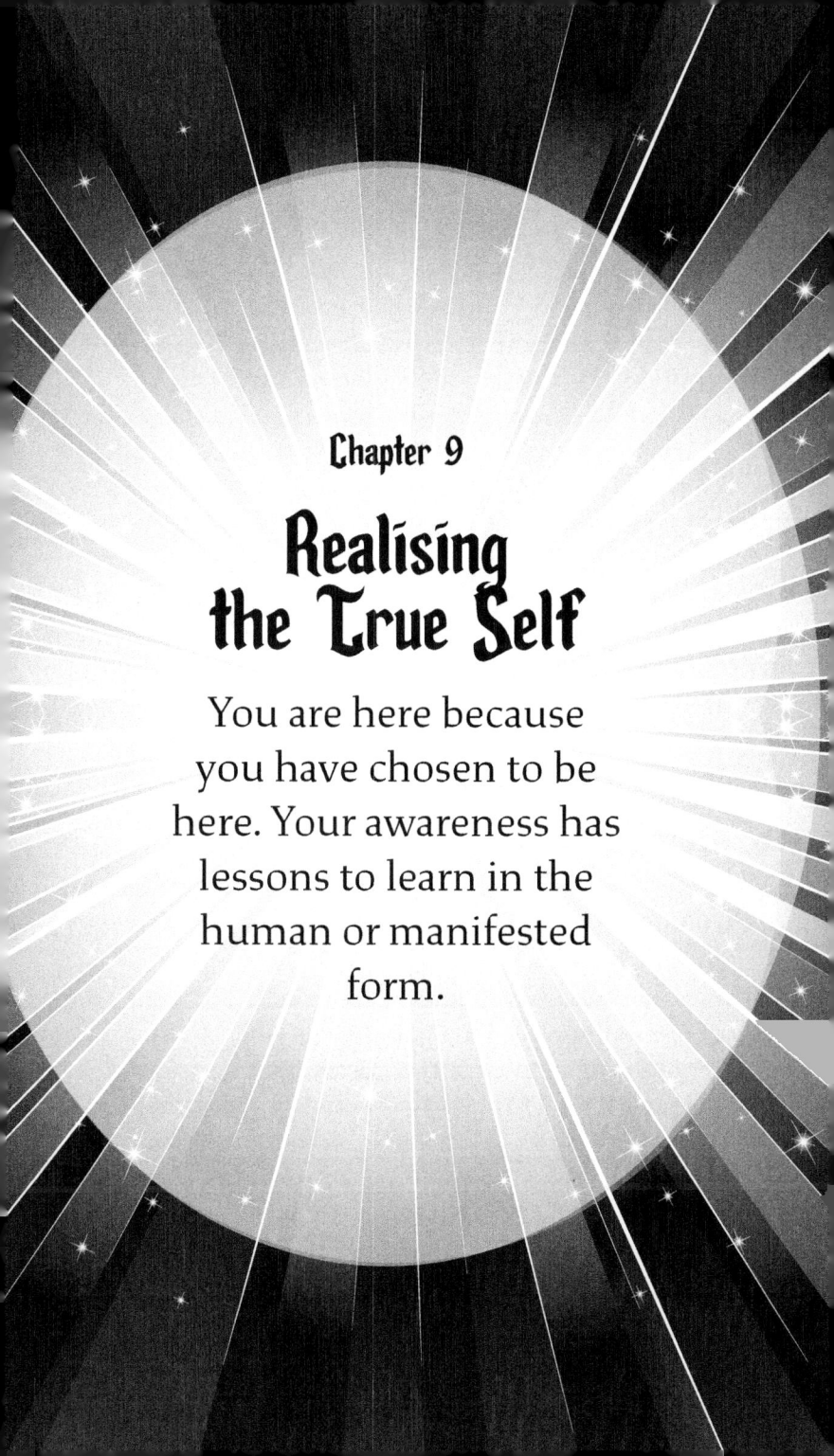

Realising the True Self

You are here because you have chosen to be here. Your awareness has lessons to learn in the human or manifested form.

Realising the True Self

Your mind regulates the external sensory system and collects data from the environment through the five senses (sight, sound, smell, taste and touch). It is responsible for the perception of an object, which you analyse and identify according to your intellect. However, intellect is completely useless unless you feed it with some data. If there is no data, intellect cannot function and without a memory data cannot be stored.

It is your memory that determines how you perceive everything around you, but you only perceive a tiny percentage of the input happening at any given moment. You live in the present, processing current inputs and information from the environment. Your life is a continuous series of moments of experience. Once these moments have passed however, most are lost forever. You might think these experiences should make up the story of your life but, in reality, they do not.

The story of your life is actually written by the act of 'remembering', but if almost all your continuous moment-to-moment experiences are lost, then what is remembered? You remember everything that you experience through the five senses - and through these senses you experience some sort of feeling. These feelings then trigger a thought to which you experience as 'good' or 'bad', 'right' or 'wrong', 'happy' or 'sad' etcetera.

Sadguru Jaggi Vasudev an Indian yogi and author explains that all that you see or hear or feel through the five senses is projected in the mind and so it is not necessary that your perception and the projected image is what the reality holds. He says the entire human experience is 'outward-bound' just as the sense objects are also outward bound. He further says: "Your memory is a complex internal mechanism, solely responsible for your perception, cognition, and intelligence. You are a living being permeated with the substance of memory not just in your head region but your entire body and around you. Every cell in the body has a phenomenal memory – not just of this life but of millions of years. Your body clearly remembers how your forefathers were a million years ago. If you look at your body, you will realise what an incredibly complex chemical factory it is."

Your body is made up of approximately 40 trillion cells. Every cell in your body has a memory and reacts in very real literal ways to the memories from this life and previous lives. Modern science teaches you that your cells contain DNA which are the blueprint for the complete design of your physical bodies. They also hold the blueprint for your emotional, mental, and spiritual state. Your cells remember who you have been in past lives and all that has been in this life right up to the present day (hence the term 'cellular memory'). So, as you change and grow in any aspect of your lives, your cells are constantly updating your personal data. Cells also retain the information of all life experiences that has been absorbed from genetic heritage, so nothing ever experienced, whether positive or negative escapes being programmed.

Cells are constantly growing and dying and they are the ultimate reflection of how the universe works. The universe is constantly changing and constantly transforming and so are your cells. Sadguru Jaggi Vasudev said: "There is undeniably a profound intelligence managing this great chemical dance. But do you think you will ever be able to conduct this chemical dance intellectually? You cannot manage a single cell in your body that way! It is pure intelligence, and like cosmic intelligence simply just there. Everything happens because of it. It does not function out of memory – it simply just functions in a way that is call cosmos a living mind. It connects to the basis of creation within you. It connects you with your consciousness".

The cosmic intelligence is the ultimate consciousness, it is where God or the Divine self is known. Remembrance of God or self-remembering happens at the level of the cosmic mind, which is the ultimate in consciousness. God or Divine self is known when you become completely integrated with the ultimate consciousness.

You are, therefore, totality itself - the ultimate consciousness where God or the Divine self is known. You do not have to become Divine you have only to discover your divinity. It is really a matter of recognition. The truth is veiled, and it is there to be unveiled. Divinity is not to be achieved but rather unveiled and recognised. What is it that veils it? It is your own forgetfulness and your unconsciousness which covers the truth.

God or the Divine self is your inner life force, your true motivation for living. It is what powers you and makes you wonder. It is the soul light at your core

Realising the True Self

that has chosen to incarnate now. It is the part of you that is aware. You are here because you have chosen to be here. Your awareness has lessons to learn in the human or manifested form.

Your physical body is therefore a vessel for your God or Divine self, which is pure love and light.

As you peel away all the conditioning and belief systems that limit you, you'll have greater access to your God or Divine self. This is the real you, your true essence and the guiding light of your soul - the part of you that is still connected with the universal energy source. It is the part of you that holds all memories of your past lives and that which holds your soul's journey and holds all knowledge.

You need to be awakened to the realisation that you are beyond time and space and beyond form and formlessness. You are that which is beyond the mind and beyond every concept of 'you' as a single identity.

The cosmic intelligence surrounds you, lives inside of you and is 'breathing' you right now. And every atom in the universe is connected to the highest source of love and life.

It is you that manifests and experiences reality as an extension of your every thought and intention. You are therefore the very Creator of your reality. Your body is a vehicle that the Creator is perceiving and experiencing life through. Everything that is seen, and unseen are just thought forms inside of the cosmic intelligence. Your reality is a construct just as ALL realities are constructs.

Deepak Chopra said, "There is no such thing as a body, mind or universe - these are human constructs for modes of knowing an experience. Consciousness is interacting with itself and having an experience.

Nothing really happens outside of consciousness, and that which you call a physical world is called a human construct. Every living sentient being is a living consciousness having an experience in an infinite consciousness that it is creating. Everything given a name to is a human construct. No system of thought can give you access to reality, you must go to the source of thought, which is consciousness itself, therefore, you need to wake up to that which is having an experience.

If you are asked who remembers your childhood or anything in the past, you say "I" remember. This is because "I" is the awareness that is having the experience. And "I" knows that it's having an experience because it remembers.

Experience disappears because it keeps transforming, but the "I" that is present is always the same. An experience is in time, but consciousness itself is not in time.

The "I" is not in the body but having an experience through the sensory perceptions. The "I" modifies itself into the experience that is a human construct called mind, body, and universe. The "I" is immortal".

When you merge with God or the Divine Self it paves the path towards spiritual ascension.

You are not the physical body or the mind, you are the life force that is immortal. Life energy doesn't disintegrate - it merges with the universe.

This is a self-realisation that allows you to understand and evaluate your real self. When you know the "I", you take charge of your thoughts, feelings, and actions that guide your behaviour. You become aware that there is something more than what you see, what you know about yourself and your existence.

You come to the realisation that you are not mere body or the mind or the senses, but the inner self, which is permanent, eternal and infinite that shares the same consciousness as that of God or the Divine. You learn how your actions have consequences and how your desires and senses bind you to your actions. You also understand the universal principle of cause and effect. You know your actions, both good and bad come back to you in the future, helping you to learn from your life's lessons.

This could be called 'karma', which is one of the natural laws of the mind, just as gravity is a law of matter. It automatically creates the appropriate future experience in response to the current action. You create your own destiny through your thoughts and actions. Whatever karma you are experiencing in your life is just what you need now - and when you connect karma with wisdom it can be the greatest catalyst for spiritual growth.

It is quite possible that karma is the result of the actions you have committed in your previous lives. Your actions and thoughts from your past lives could also influence who you are today. In other words, the life you are living at present could be a result of the ways you have lived your life in the past. Your soul will keep reincarnating until you have resolved all your karma. You should identify recurring situations in your life, acknowledge those situations, and then deal with them.

Vedanta believes that karma is stored in the 'Jiva' or the 'individual soul'. Karma can be stored from previous lives and new karma is generated throughout every moment of your existence. It is your chakras, however, that store the karma for this lifetime.

Chakras are your subtle energy centres through which consciousness transforms into matter. Karma distorts that flow of consciousness, causing you to experience an illusory world. Clearing Karma helps you to step out of the illusion.

Vedanta also adds that, "Nothing happens to you, it happens for you!"

The word 'karma' comes from the Sanskrit verb 'kri' which means 'to do'. Although karma means 'action', it also means the result of action. Whatever acts you have performed and whatever thoughts you have thought have created an impression, both in your mind and in the universe around you. The universe gives back to you that which you have given to it.

You have created through your own thoughts and actions the life that you are leading today, and you have the power to create the life that you will live tomorrow. Whether you like it or not, whether you want to take responsibility or not, that is what you are doing every step of the way.

No matter what happens in your day-to-day life, you should always try to remain the 'observer'. When you remain the observer, your mind doesn't get stuck with the repetitive cycle of life, because you experience life in the moment with absolute clarity.

Life is just a process, and you are continually creating karma with your thoughts and actions.

If you can detach from your thoughts and actions that you identify with, karma can be transcended.

This means transcending the self, going beyond your own identity and understanding that you are a small part of something bigger. It means moving forward and identifying with something greater than yourself. At the height of self-transcendence, your own needs may be put aside, to a great extent, in favour of service to others or to some spiritual higher force outside the personal self.

William Meader, a teacher of esoteric philosophy, explains that you are a 'interdimensional beings' experiencing life not only on the physical plane but emotionally, mentally, and intuitively. On a spiritual level your soul wants to express itself by providing a service to others. This means you soul needs to cooperate with the three parts of the personality which are on an emotional, mental, and physical level. The personality is what dominates, and it is where ego arises. Slowly, over many incarnations the soul connects with the ego, creating a communication bridge that links the soul with the personality. In addition, another bridge is formed from the soul to something which is called the 'Monad' or 'life above', this bridge is called the 'Antahkarana'. This is a structure that does not exist naturally; it is built over many incarnations. To strengthen this bridge there are three processes that are integrated into the fabric of a spiritually minded person's day to day life. The first is to study to build a higher mind, as the soul is found on a higher mental plane. The second is heartfelt service, because the more you can commit to serving something beyond yourself, the more you can facilitate building a bridge - and the third is meditation. Where you are on the spiritual path will determine how much of the antahkarana is constructed.

He mentions that antahkarana is a conduit, a connection between your intelligent mind and the higher levels of consciousness; it exists for the purpose of bridging the mundane to the spiritual. It makes possible the realisation of wisdom and guidance that transcends the rational thinking processes of the personality.

He also explains that the personality can be transcended during meditation, and you can experience the soul directly (even if for just a few moments). When the meditation ends, a strand of subtle substance is carried from the soul to the personality. This strand becomes a part of the bridge. Therefore, each meditation has the power to strengthen the antahkarana by adding filaments to it. In this way the antahkarana is built.

To further build the antahkarana you could provide a service to others, which indicates that you are thinking beyond your own needs. You begin to resonate to a higher form of love—a love that is widely inclusive, yet impersonal. It indicates (to the soul) that the personality is beginning to demonstrate a willingness to let go of independent tendencies, to be guided instead by a more altruistic motive.

The soul seeks to condition the mind of the personality into realising that beneath the apparent 'separateness' of things there is instead, a profound oneness, an interconnectedness of all things. The soul's mission is to merge and unite itself with the monad, which is in fact its own source and highest spiritual essence.

Activities

Write down what you remember about your story. What struggles have occurred to create the story of your life? What lessons are you experiencing right now? Your lessons and experiences are unique to you because it compels you to evolve, otherwise you become stagnant.

Start to notice your breathing, your heartbeat, your thoughts and emotions. This is life functioning as the individual you call "I." reconnect with your authentic nature by honouring the values which point you toward your true self.

When you know the "I", you take charge of your thoughts, feelings, and actions that guide your behaviour. You become aware that there is something more than what you see, what you know about yourself and your existence. You come to the realisation that you are not the mere body, mind or the senses, but the inner self, which is permanent, eternal, and infinite and which shares the same consciousness as that of God or the Divine.

Awaken to the realisation that you are beyond time and space. Also, you are beyond form. You are that which is beyond the mind and beyond every concept of 'you'.

If 'you' start to focus on the NOW it will help you understand and experience the formless nature of creation. What seems to be 'real' or have inherent existence is merely a constant state of change that is creating illusions of appearances that seem to be real or solid from the viewpoint of your mind.

Start to 'feel' the world around you and notice any sounds, sights, and sensations. Also, feel the presence of others, their emotions, thoughts, or energy. Do this often and build your subtle senses as this will make you more sensitive to the messages that register in your consciousness.

Understand that you transcend the body because you are not centred in the body. You are boundless and infinite consciousness that contains the body.

See the bigger picture by monitoring your actions from a greater awareness standpoint. This means noticing your actions and where they are coming from, whether it a place of transcendence or ego.

Identify with the recurring situations in your life, acknowledge those situations, and deal with them. Also, start to take personal responsibility for what is happening to you and make the changes today.

Meditate on the 'OM' sound by repeating it, either out loud or internally. The personality can transcend during meditation, and you can experience the soul directly (even if for just a few moments).

Identify with something greater than yourself and endeavour to be of service to others. Because, on a spiritual level your soul wants to express itself by providing a service to others.

Chapter 10

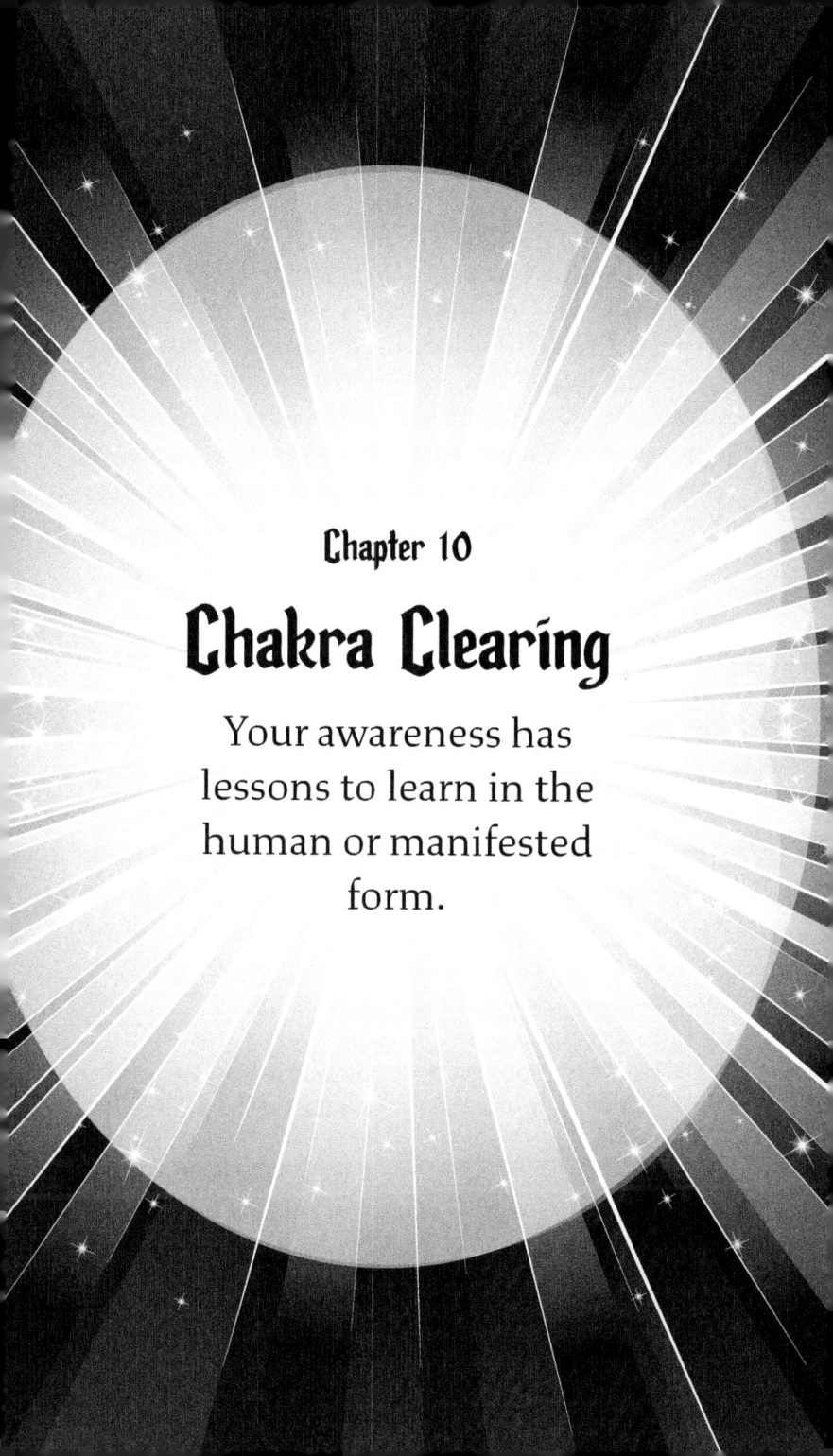

Chakra Clearing

Your awareness has lessons to learn in the human or manifested form.

Chakra Clearing

Karma is the essence of actions and actions follow the law of cause and effect. If you apply the law of cause and effect, you'll become more in harmony with your life. One way to become more in harmony with your life is through something called 'chakra clearing'. I mentioned in the last chapter that Vedanta believes that it's your chakras that store the karma for this lifetime. Chakras are your subtle energy centres through which consciousness transforms into matter.

You can work with consciousness directly by clearing your chakras to help build the antahkarana that is a part of your spiritual anatomy i.e., the soul's anatomy. It is the connection between your mind and your Divine self

The antahkarana is also called the 'rainbow bridge', which is responsible for conditioning your existence in line with divine purpose and plan. The rainbow bridge derives its name from the fusion of all the colours of the seven rays. The bridge eventually brings about a relationship between your mind and the Divine self. Like a spider that builds a web, so you, too, weave the connecting threads out of your own being that link the outer and inner worlds.

The seven colours of the rainbow and the seven chakras help you to access your Divine self. Here are the seven chakras:

—» Root Chakra (Red) - Physical Manifestation
—» Sacral Chakra (Orange) - Karmic Relations
—» Solar Plexus Chakra (Yellow) - Identity and Ego
—» Heart Chakra (Green) - Life Thread (silver cord)

—» Third Eye Chakra (Indigo) - Consciousness Thread
—» Throat Chakra (Blue) - Creative Thread
—» Crown Chakra (Violet) - Oneness

Root Chakra (Red) - Physical manifestation
This chakra is linked to the unconscious mind, where your actions and experiences from past lives are stored. According to Karmic Law, this chakra contains the course of your future destiny. This chakra is also the foundation for the development of your personality.

According to Sankhya philosophy the universe consists of two realities - human consciousness and a phenomenal realm of matter. The root chakra represents the birth of human consciousness and the four petals of the root chakra lotus symbolises the four aspects of a human mind and these are:

'Manas' the thinking aspect of mind.

'Buddhi' the intellectual analysis and discrimination aspect of mind.

'Chitta' the memory storage aspect of the mind including storage of emotional impressions.

'Ahamkara' (ego) the aspect of mind that is identifying itself with the human body (including the mind; so, mind-body complex).

Antahkarana is the combined aspects of all of the above: Manas, Buddhi, Chitta and Ahamkara. The four functions of mind are described in the Upanishads which is commonly referred to as Vedanta, where the concepts of Brahman (ultimate reality) and Atman (soul, self) are central ideas that are looked at as a wheel with four spokes. The centre of the hub never moves, which is the Self, on which the wheel of the mind seems to rotate, therefore the Self seems to operate in the apparent manifestation through the four functions of mind.

And the root chakra is the centre where reality is manifested through the four functions of the mind.

It also where the Kundalini (the life force) sleeps, waiting to be liberated. Once liberated it will give you the power to manifest anything in the material world. This life force is an energy that connects everything that exists and you are taking in this energy at every moment. This energy flows through everything. It is responsive to the four functions of the mind (manas, buddhi, chitta and ahamkara). It's a universal concept for a powerful and enlightening force which generates a profound state of consciousness.

It's very important to clear and balance this chakra before balancing the others as this is where you draw your life force energy from, to support every other chakra.

You come to this world through the root chakras of your mother and everything you try to create and manifest in life finds completion through the root chakra energy first.

When your root chakra is healthy, you will find peace - that is always here in the present moment - easier to connect to. The main idea is to work at growing your 'roots' in a safe and comfortable environment with everything you need to survive. This means sufficient food, water and shelter.

Sacral Chakra (Orange) - Karmic Relations

Karma is the accumulation of your thoughts, intentions, emotions and actions from this particular life as well as from your previous lifetimes. It gets carried forward from one life to the next, therefore, its important to clear your karma in this lifetime so the cycle doesn't continue.

This is why karmic relations are formed to complete an unfinished deed, business, or an emotional trauma. They are like mirrors that help you realise the implications of your undesirable behaviour that maybe wasn't noticeable previously.

Every karmic relation that you create from the casual to the most intimate has a purpose, no matter how painful, to help you become more consciously aware of your karma and yourself. Some relationships are necessarily difficult because it makes you learn about your own limitations. This, in turn, helps you learn how to overcome obstacles, let go of emotional blockages and walk the path towards spiritual consciousness.

Clearing the sacral chakra helps to express and understand your emotions. It's the chakra of pleasure, allowing you to enjoy life through your five senses. And it encourages you to remain flexible in your feelings and emotions.

When it's blocked it can make you feel out of touch with yourself and those around you. It can make you feel trapped in your emotions and unable to express them clearly.

It can also affect your relationships with others, as well as your zest for life. And make it difficult to express your emotions clearly.

In order to build the antahkarana it's important to have healthy relationships with others. It should be your ultimate goal to settle old karmic debts and generate as much positive karma as possible. It's important to identify with the karma that is causing you to endure the same obstacles. The only way to do this is to take different actions and remain aware of your thoughts and intentions.

Solar Plexus Chakra (Yellow) - Identity and Ego

You need an identity to be able to learn to function in the world and recognise yourself as a unique distinct person. Your identity changes once you connect with your soul, it becomes less important. What becomes important is the ability to express your soul, by letting go of any attachment to a fixed personal identity. Instead, you can identify with the dynamic presence of your being. Your personal identity perceives everything as separate, whilst your soul knows that the essence of everything is interconnected.

It's important to become self-aware and to master the art of recognising your ego. Also, understand that ego is a functional part of your mind. The challenge of being aware of your ego is that your mind has been programmed to wrongly believe that the ego is you.

It's your beliefs and behaviours that contribute to the foundational makeup of the ego. It's your cultural and moral programming, attitude, definition of acceptable behaviour, conduct, and standards.

Every successful accomplishment and achievement serve to feed your ego. However, it is the soul that yearns to contribute and focus on what you're able to give, which is why giving is so fulfilling. It's important to flow with life and keep your ambition, willpower, and action, in balance.

Your ego can prevent you from growing and evolving if you are full of guilt, shame, sadness, anger or fear. This can have a significant effect on your behaviour and your actions creating karmic debt.

What helps, is to become aware of your thoughts and actions. Ask yourself if your thoughts and actions are aligned with your soul or with your ego? An ego thought starts to move into your emotional body and here it begins the journey to manifested reality. This means it goes down to the root chakra where it manifests. But manifestations here are rooted in guilt, shame, sadness, greed or fear. Whereas a higher vibrational thought moves up to the heart chakra where it can manifest in a loving manner.

Heart Chakra (Green) - Life thread (silver cord)

The life thread comes directly from the 'Monad' or the ONE. This thread anchors itself in the heart chakra during incarnation. This is the seat of life. It is often referred to as the "silver cord" because it supplies energy to the physical body. If the silver cord is severed, the physical body can no longer be sustained and dies. It provides the subtle and physical bodies with vital energy.

With an open-heart chakra, you can surrender to love and realise that you are not separated from the monad or the ONE anymore. You feel a constant connection with Divine love, because you know that you are the tool through which it gets expressed.

You see and feel the invisible connections between yourself and everyone else – the unity of the world.

In other people's actions, you can see the reflections of your own shadow side. This is because everything you notice in others is a reflection of yourself.

When you stop blaming others for your problems you start to take personal responsibility for everything that happens to you. You don't have a victim mentality anymore, therefore, you begin to recognise any negative situation as a karmic lesson that is essential for your spiritual growth and personal evolution.

This chakra is very sensitive and easily blocked when you are wounded to protect yourself from further pain. To heal this chakra, you have to practice empathy, compassion, and most importantly true forgiveness of those who may have hurt you in the past.

Third eye chakra (Indigo) - Consciousness thread
This thread extends from the soul to the mind of your personality (ego) and is seated within the brain cavity in the region of the pineal gland. Through it, you can begin to register the wisdom of the soul. Unlike the life thread, this substructure of the antahkarana does not exist naturally - it must be built.

Like a spider, you must spin your own web, connect this thread and build a rainbow bridge. The building of the antahkarana is primarily an activity of the personality, aided by the soul.

The pineal gland is considered the doorway to a higher dimension. It helps you see beyond everyday linear reality. Intentionally activating your pineal gland (or third eye) tunes you into a reality beyond the five senses.

It's through the awakening of the third eye and its corresponding pineal gland that you're able to attain an intimate connection with your soul.

Through an open and vibrant third eye, you will find your highest source of ethereal energy. A return path to the monad or the ONE.

The Greeks believed the pineal gland ruled thought, while Rene Descartes held it as the seat of the soul.

While the physical eyes perceive the physical world, the third eye sees the true world—a unified whole with an unyielding connection to the Monad or the ONE.

A blocked third eye chakra will decrease the quality of your life experience and slow down the process of your spiritual awakening as it provides you with the highest version of insight and beneficial guidance in all aspects of your life. It is where intuition can be fully recognised as your reliable inner voice or inner knowing.

The feeling of disconnection from your intuition and instinct, also known as the sixth sense, (which is your innate wisdom) can affect your response to various life experiences. It can make you feel very confused about your life purpose and the reason you are here on Earth. You are here to discover and uncover the truth and meaning of who you are.

You are currently a soul incarnated in physical form creating karma that needs to be resolved. It is possible to resolve karma by building a consciousness thread to free yourself from any karmic debt as a way to evolve. This means connecting your soul with your personality (ego), creating a communication bridge that links the soul with the personality thus leading you back to the monad or the ONE.

Willam Meader explains that building a 'higher mind', providing a heartfelt service and committing yourself to serving something beyond yourself, builds the antahkarana.

He also mentions that meditation helps to experience the soul directly (even if for just a few moments), and when the meditation ends, a strand of subtle substance is carried from the soul to the personality. This strand becomes a part of the bridge. Therefore, each meditation has the power to strengthen the antahkarana by adding filaments to it. In this way the antahkarana is built.

Throat Chakra (Blue) - Creative thread

This is where karmic thought patterns or impressions mainly manifest, therefore, self-expression and living in accordance with your higher truth will help to balance this chakra. If it is unbalanced you will not be able to express yourself clearly.

This is where the creative thread is anchored, which relates to the expression of yourself through purpose and individuality.

The throat chakra's focus is on expressing ideas clearly, gracefully and honestly. It projects your authentic creativity into the world. And when creativity is flowing freely, it provides profound spiritual truths and you are able to speak, listen, and express yourself fully. If it's not flowing freely, you'll find it difficult to align your personal vision with reality when expressing your creativity into the world.

As a creator, you draw energy from spiritual knowledge and use it to fuel your creative endeavours. That is your purpose here: to create and grow and expand your consciousness.

"After all, you are a human being created by one God, on one Earth, in complete unison. You are part and parcel of that One Primordial Being. You are cells in the body of that Great Being." (Shri Mataji Nirmala Devi)

You are made to imitate God. You create because God created first. As a human being you were made to be creative.

It is the nature of your soul to express itself in some form of creativity - and when doing this - you can sometimes lose your sense of the separate self and experience a unity with the soul. Then the soul becomes a singular life and a bridge to the monad or the ONE is created.

Crown Chakra (Violet) - Oneness

This chakra is known as 'the bridge to the cosmos'. It is the most spiritual in nature of all seven chakras. Located above the crown of the head, it acts as a centre of spirit, enlightenment, wisdom, universal consciousness and a connection to higher guidance.

When this chakra is open and functioning, it is an intimate connection to God/Source/Creator Energy. This connection is an ever-flowing wisdom of intuitive knowing of Divine inspiration. When it is blocked you can feel disconnected from the Divine, feeling separate rather than feeling in a state of 'oneness'.

This chakra deals specifically with karma that is carried over from previous lifetimes and is intrinsically connected to the path you walk and the challenges you face. It's a gateway to potential transcendence and true awakening.

You were put onto this Earth to do a certain amount of energetic clearing that requires learning lessons through life. Sometimes, these lessons get missed, because you are too busy to see them in action thus causing you to repeat the same patterns.

The purpose of your existence here on Earth is to gain correct knowledge and insight. If you do not make use of this opportunity and remain in ignorance, then after death you must again return to the world in a new body to clear all unresolved karma.

Activities

Walk barefoot in nature when you are feeling a little off-balance. This can connect you to the life force energy that flows through everything. Focus on your root chakra and find peace in the present moment.

Clear and balance the root chakra before balancing the other chakras, as this is where you draw your life force energy that supports every other chakra.

Focus and clear your sacral chakra to help express and understand your emotions. Start taking more notice of your five senses.

Learn how to overcome obstacles, let go of emotional blockages, and walk the path towards spiritual consciousness.

Create healthy relationships with others and generate as much positive karma as possible. Identify with the karma that's causing you to endure the same obstacles. You can do this by taking different actions and remaining aware of your thoughts and intentions.

Ask yourself if your thoughts are aligned with your soul, or with your ego? Are your thoughts higher vibrational thoughts that are manifesting with love or are they full of guilt, shame, sadness, greed or fear?

Open your heart chakra by surrendering to love and realise that you are not separated from the Divine. Start to feel a connection with Divine love, because you can be the tool through which it gets expressed.

Stop blaming others for your problems. Instead, take personal responsibility for everything that happens to you. Truly forgive those who may have hurt you in the past and try to have more compassion.

Start to build a 'higher mind', provide a heartfelt service and commit yourself to serving something beyond yourself.

Remember that the reason you are here on this Earth is to discover your true self, and to live in accordance with the higher truth. So, it's important to balance the throat chakra and express yourself clearly.

Know that it's the nature of your soul to express itself in some form of creativity. When doing this you will lose your sense of the separate self and instead create a unity with the soul.

Start to meditate as this will help you to experience the soul directly (even if for just a few moments).

Take the time to examine the actions that are causing you to repeat the same patterns. It's important to do a certain amount of energetic clearing that requires learning lessons through life.

Summary

You can change the quality of your life when you begin to tap into the power of your subconscious mind because you will start to notice your wise inner voice. This wise inner voice is calm and non-judgmental and it helps navigate your spiritual journey.

A spiritual journey is an inner quest to shift your conscious experience or perception of the outer world to an inner world of pure awareness or a higher state of consciousness.

This inner world can be reached by creating sacred space. This is a place you can go to mentally and emotionally in order to clear your mind, so that you can listen to your wise inner voice.

A sacred space is created in a shamanic drum circle and it is a place where you don't have to think anymore. A place where you can let go with rhythmic sound, explore your subconscious mind and enter insightful states that open access to unseen dimensions using the beat of the drum.

A shamanic drum is a tool to commune with the unseen world to effect changes in the physical world, to retrieve information from your Spirit Guides that provide you with insights. These are insights into things you must do and/or change as you pursue your own personal growth and spiritual transformation.

A spiritual transformation is all about monitoring yourself so it requires a higher level of introspection and self-awareness that changes the environment you surround yourself with.

It alters your thoughts and feelings in a way that attract situations and people to your life. This is because you are connected to everything that has an energy field. An energy field is found around every living organism such as, animals, plants, and people. This is what sustains life and provides vital energy to everything.

When universal life force energy doesn't flow properly through your subtle energy field, blockages can develop. However, it is possible to channel healing using universal life force energy to the subtle energy field by expanding consciousness.

The body's subtle energy field is a system made up of layers of vibrating energy, each of which have their own specific vibration and purpose. There are also subtle energy centres within the energy field called chakras through which consciousness transforms into matter.

Chakras are linked to the unconscious mind, where your actions and experiences from past lives are stored. They accumulate your thoughts, intentions, emotions and actions from this particular life as well as from your previous lifetimes. They are intrinsically connected to the path you walk and the challenges you face. They are a gateway to potential transcendence and true awakening so when blocked you can feel disconnected from your Divine self, feeling separate rather than in a state of 'oneness'.

Your Divine self is your inner life force, your true motivation for living. It is what powers you and gives you a sense of wonder. It is the soul light at your core that has chosen to incarnate now. It is the part of you that is aware. You are here because you have chosen to be here. Your awareness has lessons to learn in the human or manifested form.

Glossary

Altered State of Consciousness - A non-ordinary state of awareness and perception that can happen through meditation, prayer, chant, or trance.

Astrology Natal Chart - This shows the position of the sun, the moon and the planets moving through the different twelve zodiac signs and houses at the time of your birth. These positions at the time of your birth impact your personality and your life pattern.

Attuning your Energy - This means becoming more receptive to your internal energy systems and become more aware of it and in tune with it.

Authentic Self - This is who you are at the core of your being. You become your Authentic Self when your thoughts, feelings and actions are in complete alignment with your true nature.

Aura - This is an energy field which is a coloured emanation that surrounds your body or any animal or object. Every living thing has an energy field that emits vibrations which reveal its spiritual, emotional, and physical state of well-being.

Chakras - In Sanskrit, the word "Chakra" translates to 'wheel', 'circle', or 'vortex'. The chakras, which are aligned along your spine, spin and rotate in a constant clockwise motion, like a whirlpool of energy and light. Your chakras serve to circulate a universal life force energy through your subtle bodies. Each chakra has its own unique auric field which contributes to the overall auric effect around the body. The auric field is made up of seven layers which relate and correspond to the seven chakras.

Cosmic intelligence - It is not only humans, animals and plants that manifest intelligence. The Earth itself (Gaia) has an intrinsic intelligence as do all parts of the cosmos.

Earths Electromagnetic Field - This is also known as the geomagnetic field that emanates from the core of the Earth. It is interesting to know that animals, including birds and turtles, can detect the Earth's magnetic field and use the field to navigate during migration.

Expanding Awareness - In order to expand your normal level of awareness means becoming more acutely aware of the world around you both physically and energetically both in terms of observation from a rational conscious state, as well as subjective experience coming from all six senses.

God or 'Divine Self' - The essence within you or the light within your soul that has chosen to incarnate now. The eternal, infinite consciousness, free from all attachments and beyond all action. It is constant and unchanging, birthless and deathless.

Heightened Awareness - When you begin to realise that there is an inner world and that you are more than just your body or mind.

Higher Consciousness - The consciousness of 'God' or the internal awareness of your true nature as an immortal consciousness that is capable of transcending death.

Higher Vibration - This is the energy that is created by adopting positive feelings such as love, forgiveness, compassion and peace. Low vibration, in contrast, is associated with darker qualities such as hatred, fear, greed and depression.

Human Electromagnetic Field - This is part of the universal energy field that is associated with the human body. It is also sometimes called the 'Light body' which is a structure of light from higher dimensions. Like the physical body it is a vehicle for consciousness. Just as your physical body contains organs and other physical structures, your light body contains various structures made of light.

Inner-Self - A state of consciousness that can be accessed through meditation and introspection, which promotes greater self-awareness and acceptance.

Inner wisdom - Spiritual information that, with practice, you can access within yourself and which emanates from a higher consciousness.

Interdimensional Beings - As a human being you exist in the first, second and third dimensions but you also have the innate potential to extend into the fourth, fifth, sixth and seventh dimensions and beyond as you develop your higher mind and expand your consciousness. Other spiritual entities inhabit these higher dimensional realms.

Portals - The term used to describe energy based 'doorways', 'gates' or 'entrances' to other realities and dimensions

Raising your Energy Level - Deliberately choosing to raise your own personal vibrational rate by positively increasing your emotional, mental, and physical state of awareness.

Sacred Space - Creating of locating a special place to develop your spiritual awareness by taking 'time out' to focus on your own self-development. A sacred space is somewhere to experience a depth, richness, and sense of meaning that usually escapes your fast-paced everyday life.

Self-Awareness - This is about learning how to consciously connect with - and understand more - your own characteristics, feelings, emotions, motives and desires.

Shamanism - A religious practice that involves a practitioner who is able to interact with the spirit world through altered states of consciousness such as trance.

Shamanic Drum - A percussion tool used to assist travel to the spirit world. The drumstick creates the beat that induces the trance enabling passage from one world to another.

Glossary

Spiritual Awakening - This is a new revelation, breakthrough or sudden enlightenment that happens to us on our life journey. It is essentially a newfound awareness of spiritual reality and a realisation that you are not separate from creation, but an intrinsic part of it.

Spiritual Ascension - This is about reaching new insights and truths and transcending old limiting habits, beliefs, mindset and ways of being. It is when your awareness expands on the physical, mental, emotional and spiritual level.

Spirit Animal - Known as a 'power animal' or 'spirit guide' these are spiritual teachers or messengers in animal form. Your spirit animal guides you through the journey of life, showing you how to find the answers to life's problem within yourself.

Spirit Guides - These can be angels, animals, mythical creature, ancestors, ancient gods or goddesses, otherworldly entities, or interdimensional beings. They are always there to help and guide you in any situation; implanting a thought to assist in keeping you safe and protected.

Spiritual Journey - A personal quest that we all undertake consciously or unconsciously to reconnect with our soul, our authentic self, our life purpose and our true nature.

Spirit World - A realm that exists across many dimensions that is inhabited by spirits or various spiritual manifestations.

Transcending the Self - A realisation or revelation that you are one small part of a greater whole and part of a unity consciousness.

Ultimate Consciousness - The consciousness awareness of your higher self, the wider universe and God. It's something we can all achieve if we learn to shift our level of consciousness.

Universal Consciousness - A single consciousness pervading the entire universe. Its inherent nature is All-Knowing, All-Powerful, All-Creative and All-Present.

Universal Intelligence - The universe is essentially 'mind' which is an intelligent energy force that can be tapped into if you develop the consciousness to do so. The entire world of matter and everything you experience with your five senses is all just energy.

Universal Truth - There are many universally recognised life truths that affect everyone in some form or another regardless of religious, cultural, ethnic and geographical differences. For instance - all human beings' experience stress, hardships and the need to be loved or accepted in some form.

Universal Wisdom - Awareness of yourself and your connection to all material and spiritual forms of knowledge on multiple planes of existence.

Wise Inner Voice - Your higher consciousness communicating with you through your intuition.

Recommended Reading

THE SEVEN STAGES OF THE SOUL
by Joe St Clair

SURFER OF THE UNIVERSAL WAVE
by Piper Cheyanne

THE UNTETHERED SOUL:
THE JOURNEY BEYOND YOURSELF
by Michael A. Singer

THE SPIRITUAL SECRETS OF
HAPPINESS AND SUCCESS
by Andrew C Walton

THE POWER OF
YOUR SUBCONSIOUS MIND
by Dr. Joseph Murphy

A PATH WITH HEART
by Jack Kornfield

SACRED DRUMMING
by Steven Ash

THE KYBALION
by Three Initiates

THE SECRET
By Rhonda Byrne

HEAL YOURSELF BY
CLEARING THE CHAKRAS
by Kim Michaels

Acknowledgements

I would like to thank Noel Williams and Piper Cheyanne for making this book possible. Also, for the infinite wisdom that gave me the ability to write this book. It is a wonderful gift if you just take the time to listen to your wise inner voice.

About the Author

Louise was born with her psychic abilities already in evidence and has been able to see and communicate with spirits for as long as she can remember. By the time she was an adolescent her connection to the 'spirit world' began to overwhelm her as her abilities started to expand, making it increasingly difficult for her to deal with her day-to-day environment. The lines between her own thoughts and the emotional energy of others, whether in body or not, had started to become blurred. Over time though, she began to gain more control over her expanding awareness and eventually taught herself to master her extraordinary psychic abilities.

Later, working in her local spiritualist centre as a professional medium, she completed a 'Spiritualist National Union' healing course at the age of twenty-one. This enabled her to provide healing to people at many other spiritual centres as well as setting up groups to help other psychics and mediums to develop their own abilities.

In 2018 Louise started attending 'Shamanic drum circles' that completely transformed her life. These circles introduced her to many new and powerful experiences that helped her enter into other states of consciousness which further awakened her latent abilities. In addition, they helped her to communicate with her inner-self and connect to the roots of her deepest thoughts and emotions. This method of introspection has served to deepen and increase her knowledge and understanding of what spiritual wisdom really means.

Louise can be reached at
zakrzewskalouise320@gmail.com

Printed in Great Britain
by Amazon